Synthesis Lectures on Operations Research and Applications

Series Editor

James Cochran, AMES, USA

This series focuses on the use of advanced analytics in both industry and scientific research to advance the quality of decisions and processes. Written by international experts, modern applications and methodologies are utilized to help researchers and students alike to improve their use of analytics. Classical and cutting-edge topics are presented and explored with a focus on utilization and application across a range in practical situations.

Serhat Gul • Özlem Karsu

Chemotherapy Appointment Scheduling

Addressing Uncertainty and Fairness

Springer

Serhat Gul
Department of Industrial Engineering
TED University
Ankara, Türkiye

Özlem Karsu
Department of Industrial Engineering
Bilkent University
Ankara, Türkiye

ISSN 2770-6303 ISSN 2770-6311 (electronic)
Synthesis Lectures on Operations Research and Applications
ISBN 978-3-032-11551-5 ISBN 978-3-032-11552-2 (eBook)
https://doi.org/10.1007/978-3-032-11552-2

This Springer imprint is published by the registered company Springer Nature Switzerland AG
The registered company address is: Gewerbestrasse 11, 6330 Cham, Switzerland

We dedicate this book to our families, and to all chemotherapy patients and care providers.

Preface

The increasing demand for chemotherapy services underscores the importance of effective scheduling in outpatient chemotherapy units (OCUs). The inherent uncertainty in treatment durations necessitates the development of stochastic optimization models for both phases of chemotherapy scheduling—planning treatment days and setting appointment times. While this book touches on the former phase, its primary emphasis is on chemotherapy appointment scheduling, a topic that has received significant attention from researchers in recent years. Two-stage stochastic mixed-integer programming formulations are introduced as powerful tools for generating daily appointment schedules. Throughout the book, we present different formulations that incorporate key aspects such as fairness, care coordination, nurse satisfaction, nursing care delivery approaches, treatment quality, and operational efficiency.

Among these aspects, fairness receives particular emphasis. We discuss the challenges of quantifying fairness, representing it through mathematical functions, and integrating these functions into stochastic programming models for chemotherapy appointment scheduling. Using real-world data from an OCU, we conduct a case study to generate appointment schedules based on the discussed models. The resulting schedules are analyzed with respect to operational efficiency, patient equity, and workload distribution, and are compared with baseline schedules from practice.

This book is designed to benefit a diverse audience. For researchers, it provides a comprehensive overview of state-of-the-art stochastic optimization models and fairness measures in chemotherapy scheduling, as well as open research directions. Practitioners in oncology service delivery can gain insights into how advanced scheduling models can improve patient flow, resource utilization, equity, and staff satisfaction. For graduate students newly entering this field, the book serves as both an introduction to fundamental concepts and a guide to advanced modeling approaches, equipping them with the tools to carry out impactful research in healthcare operations.

Ankara, Turkey
September 2025

Serhat Gul
Özlem Karsu

Acknowledgments We gratefully acknowledge our co-authors in earlier studies that have provided a basis for this book: Prof. Melih Çelik, Prof. Tonguç Ünlüyurt, Dr. Nur Banu Altinpulluk, Dr. Sırma Karakaya, Dr. Günsu Dağıstanlı Çallı, Batuhan Çelik, and Ege Dilan Özyüksel. Their contributions have been invaluable in shaping the research presented here. We also extend our thanks to Hacettepe University Oncology Hospital for providing the dataset used in our earlier studies, which continues to serve as a valuable resource in this book.

Declarations

Competing Interests The authors have no conflicts of interest to declare that are relevant to the content of this book.

Ethics Approval No ethics approval was required.

Contents

1 Introduction: Background Information on Chemotherapy Delivery 1
1.1 Cancer and Chemotherapy 1
1.2 Chemotherapy Treatment Delivery 4
1.3 Critical Resources in Chemotherapy Process 6
References 7

2 Chemotherapy Scheduling 9
2.1 Key Challenges: Uncertainty, Care Coordination, Fairness 9
2.2 Chemotherapy Treatment Planning 10
2.3 Chemotherapy Appointment Scheduling 11
2.3.1 Setting Patient Appointment Times 11
2.3.2 Nurse Assignment 13
2.3.3 Chair Assignment 14
2.3.4 Consideration of Uncertainty 14
2.3.5 Performance Measures 15
2.3.6 Modeling Approach 18
2.3.7 Solution Methods 18
References 19

3 Uncertainty in Chemotherapy Scheduling 21
3.1 Scope and Sources of Uncertainty 21
3.2 Modeling Chemotherapy Scheduling Problem Under Uncertainty 23
3.2.1 Base Model 23
3.2.2 Nurse Workload Balance 26
3.2.3 Instantaneous Nurse Workload 27
3.2.4 Nursing Care Flexibility 30
3.2.5 Coordinating Oncologist Consultation Appointments with Chemotherapy Treatment Appointments 31
References 37

4 Fairness in Chemotherapy Scheduling 39
4.1 Fairness in Healthcare: Key Concepts 39
4.1.1 Input Fairness vs. Outcome Fairness 40
4.1.2 To Whom to Be Fair? 41
4.1.3 How to Achieve Fair Allocations? 42
4.2 Quantifying Fairness in Healthcare Delivery 42
4.2.1 Well-known Fairness Functions Used in Service Systems 43
4.2.2 Fairness in Stochastic Settings 49
4.3 Incorporating Fairness Criteria into Chemotherapy Scheduling Models 51
4.3.1 Gini Coefficient 51
4.3.2 Rawlsian 52
4.3.3 Equity and Efficiency Encouraging Metric (EEEM) 52
References 55

5 Case Study 57
5.1 Scheduling Practices and Dataset from the OCU at Hacettepe Oncology Hospital 57
5.2 Example Scheduling Solutions 58
5.3 Improvement over the Baseline Schedule 61
References 63

6 Conclusion and Future Directions 65
6.1 Conclusion 65
6.2 Directions for Future Work 69
References 71

Acronyms

OCU	Outpatient Chemotherapy Unit
CAS	Chemotherapy Appointment Scheduling
IV	Intravenous
CBC	Complete Blood Count
Chem-7	Basic Metabolic Panel (Seven-Parameter Metabolic Profile)
IP	Integer Programming
MIP	Mixed-Integer Programming
SMIP	Stochastic Mixed-Integer Programming
DES	Discrete-Event Simulation
MAPE	Mean Absolute Percent Error
OR	Operations Research
MS	Management Science
OECD	Organization for Economic Co-operation and Development
MAD	Mean Absolute Deviation
SoPD	Sum of Pairwise Differences
OWA	Ordered Weighted Averaging
GL	Generalized Lorenz
EEEM	Equity and Efficiency Encouraging Metric
TWT	Total Waiting Time
WT	Waiting Time
CWT	Cumulative Waiting Time
CSoWT	Cumulative Share of Waiting Time
CSoPP	Cumulative Share of Patient Population
OT	Overtime

1 Introduction: Background Information on Chemotherapy Delivery

Abstract

As cancer incidence continues to rise globally, alongside improvements in treatment outcomes, the demand for oncology—and particularly chemotherapy—services is increasing rapidly. This growing demand underscores the importance of effective scheduling, especially in outpatient chemotherapy units. In this chapter, we first provide background information on the prevalence of cancer and its treatment, followed by an overview of the different types of chemotherapy and their modes of administration. We then introduce the concept of chemotherapy regimens and their role in structuring treatment cycles. Next, we outline the patient flow during a typical chemotherapy visit in an outpatient setting, highlighting each step of the treatment delivery process. Finally, we examine the critical resources involved in chemotherapy care and their roles in treatment process.

1.1 Cancer and Chemotherapy

Cancer is the second leading cause of death worldwide, according to the World Health Organization. In 2022, nearly 10 million deaths were attributed to cancer, accounting for 1 in 6 deaths globally. Approximately 1 in 5 individuals develop cancer during their lifetime [13]. In the United States, cancer is projected to account for over 2 million new cases annually and approximately 1700 deaths per day [4].

Looking ahead, global cancer cases are expected to rise dramatically, with over 35 million new cases predicted by 2050—an increase of 77% from the estimated 20 million cases in 2022 [6]. Despite this alarming trend, significant progress has been made in reducing cancer mortality. Advances in treatment and earlier diagnosis for certain cancers have contributed to a steady decline in the cancer death rate, which has decreased by

S. Gul, Ö. Karsu, *Chemotherapy Appointment Scheduling*, Synthesis Lectures on Operations Research and Applications, https://doi.org/10.1007/978-3-032-11552-2_1

1.7% per year over the past decade [4]. However, the increasing prevalence of cancer, coupled with advances in treatment, has created a growing demand for oncology services that far exceeds current service capacity. This mismatch has led to record-high wait times for cancer care, as evidenced recently in the UK [2].

The type of treatment selected for a cancer patient depends on several factors, including the type of cancer (e.g., lung, breast, colorectal) and its stage. Cancer staging is determined based on characteristics such as tumor size and the extent to which the cancer has spread beyond its original site. If the cancer remains limited to the layer of cells where it originated, it is referred to as *in situ*. Once cancer cells invade beyond the original tissue layer, the disease is considered invasive and categorized as local, regional, or distant depending on the extent of invasion. In addition to describing the stage based on location, oncologists often use a numerical staging system, ranging from 0 to 4, to classify most cancers.

Chemotherapy is a widely used cancer treatment that can be administered at any stage of the disease. Its primary purpose is to destroy cancer cells and prevent them from multiplying. Depending on the treatment goals, chemotherapy can be classified into four main types: curative, adjuvant, neoadjuvant, and palliative therapy. Curative chemotherapy is used as the primary treatment with the goal of completely eradicating cancer. Adjuvant chemotherapy is administered after surgery or radiation therapy to eliminate any remaining cancer cells and reduce the risk of recurrence. Neoadjuvant chemotherapy is given before surgery or radiation therapy to shrink a tumor, making it easier to remove or treat. Palliative chemotherapy is used when curing the cancer is not possible. Instead, it aims to relieve symptoms and improve quality of life. The choice of chemotherapy approach depends on factors such as the cancer type, its location and stage, and the patient's overall health [3].

Chemotherapy is typically administered as a systemic therapy, meaning that the drug circulates throughout the entire body to target cancer cells. Systemic chemotherapy, which has been in use since the 1940s, can be delivered through various methods [18]. The most common method is intravenous (IV) infusion, where the drugs are administered directly into a vein through a catheter. Another option is oral chemotherapy, in which patients take the drugs as pills or capsules. Chemotherapy can also be given via injection, where the drugs are delivered using a needle. Lastly, topical chemotherapy involves applying a cream containing the drug directly to the skin.

While some cancers can be treated with a single chemotherapy drug, it is more common to use a combination of drugs in a specific order or regimen. Using multiple drugs together can enhance their effectiveness by destroying a larger number of cancer cells. Additionally, combination chemotherapy helps reduce the risk of cancer cells developing resistance to a single drug. The selection of drug combinations, dosages, and treatment schedules for a patient is often guided by insights from previous clinical trials. However, this decision also depends on various personal factors, including the type and stage of cancer, the patient's age and overall health, as well as prior treatments received.

Chemotherapy drugs are strong medications with a narrow therapeutic window due to safety and efficacy concerns. Administering doses that are too low may leave the cancer untreated, while excessively high doses can cause severe side effects—such as bleeding, diarrhea, hair loss, nausea, and vomiting—by damaging healthy cells in the body. Therefore, an oncologist must carefully determine the appropriate dosage. Typically, doses are calculated based on a patient's weight and/or height. Since children are more sensitive to these drugs, their dosages may require further adjustments even after accounting for these parameters.

Chemotherapy is administered in structured intervals known as cycles, each of which may span multiple weeks. Patients undergo several cycles throughout their treatment. On designated treatment days within a cycle, one or more chemotherapy drugs are administered. These treatment days are followed by rest periods to allow the body to recover, as chemotherapy affects not only cancer cells but also healthy cells. In some cases, drugs may be administered daily or every other day over an extended period before a rest phase begins. This approach ensures that certain drugs reach their peak effectiveness when given in consecutive doses.

A chemotherapy regimen specifies which drug will be administered, on which day, and at what dosage. The regimen selected for a patient is determined based on the type and stage of cancer, as well as the patient's overall health. For example, *Stanford-V* is one of the chemotherapy regimens used for the treatment of Hodgkin lymphoma. The cycle length for the *Stanford-V* regimen is typically 28 days. In a study conducted by the University of Nebraska Medical Center, the regimen was applied over 3 cycles [1]. The regimen schedule for a given cycle is provided in Table 1.1. Note that Prednisone is taken orally, while the remaining drugs are given intravenously (IV). According to this regimen, patients receive IV drugs on days 1, 8, 15, 16, and 22, and take oral drugs every other day throughout the cycle.

Strict adherence to the treatment regimen is crucial. Administering chemotherapy early can increase side effects due to inadequate recovery time, while delays can reduce dose intensity, potentially diminishing treatment effectiveness. Studies have shown that lower dose intensity negatively impacts health outcomes [8, 19].

At the start of each cycle, patients typically undergo lab tests and/or imaging. Based on these results and a physical exam, oncologists determine whether adjustments to the chemotherapy dosage or timing are needed. Modifications may also be required if severe side effects occur.

Table 1.1 Stanford-V chemotherapy regimen schedule for a given cycle

Days	Drugs
Day 1	Doxorubicin, Vinblastine, Mechlorethamine
Day 8	Vincristine, Bleomycin
Day 15	Doxorubicin, Vinblastine, Etoposide
Day 16	Etoposide
Day 22	Vincristine, Bleomycin
Every other day	Prednisone

1.2 Chemotherapy Treatment Delivery

Chemotherapy treatment is administered in various settings based on multiple factors, including the type and dosage of the drug, hospital policies, patient insurance coverage, individual preferences, and oncologist recommendations [5]. Specifically, it may be administered in one of the following settings: (1) an outpatient chemotherapy unit (OCU), (2) a hospital, (3) an oncologist's office, or (4) at home.

Chemotherapy can be administered at home in certain cases, such as when a patient takes oral chemotherapy pills, receives care from home chemotherapy nurses provided by a hospital, or uses a portable infusion pump for continuous drug delivery [7]. However, even in these cases, a hospital visit is often necessary to initiate treatment or to administer intravenous fluids before or after chemotherapy. If chemotherapy is administered intravenously, it is typically provided in an OCU. Even when a patient requires treatment for several consecutive days, they can visit the OCU daily without needing to stay overnight in the hospital.

Some patients may require inpatient chemotherapy, staying in the hospital for several days. This may be necessary when the drug must be administered slowly under controlled conditions, when intravenous fluids are required before and after treatment, when close monitoring is needed due to patient sensitivity, or when the regimen involves multiple doses per day over consecutive days [7]. However, transitioning certain chemotherapy regimens from inpatient to outpatient care, when feasible, can reduce costs and enhance patient satisfaction. For example, a study at the University of Arizona Cancer Center found that shifting rituximab administration from an inpatient to an outpatient setting led to significant improvements in both cost and care outcomes [16].

In a typical Outpatient Chemotherapy Unit (OCU), a patient follows these key steps in a single visit (see Fig. 1.1):

- *Registration*: Patient is checked in and the relevant paperwork is completed.
- *Lab Testing*: Since chemotherapy drugs also affect healthy cells, blood tests must be conducted in the phlebotomy department to determine whether a patient is ready for their next round of treatment.
- *Oncologist Consultation*: The oncologist assesses the patient's condition by reviewing lab results and evaluating their overall health. Based on this assessment, they confirm or cancel the chemotherapy treatment for that day. If confirmed, a drug preparation order is sent to the pharmacy. Otherwise, the patient is informed of the cancellation, and their treatment is rescheduled for a later date.
- *Drug Preparation*: The pharmacy prepares the chemotherapy drugs according to the oncologist's orders. Once ready, the drugs are transported to the chemotherapy treatment area by designated staff. During this process, patients remain in the waiting area until the prepared drugs are delivered. However, they may experience additional waiting time if a nurse or chemotherapy chair is unavailable. Once these resources become

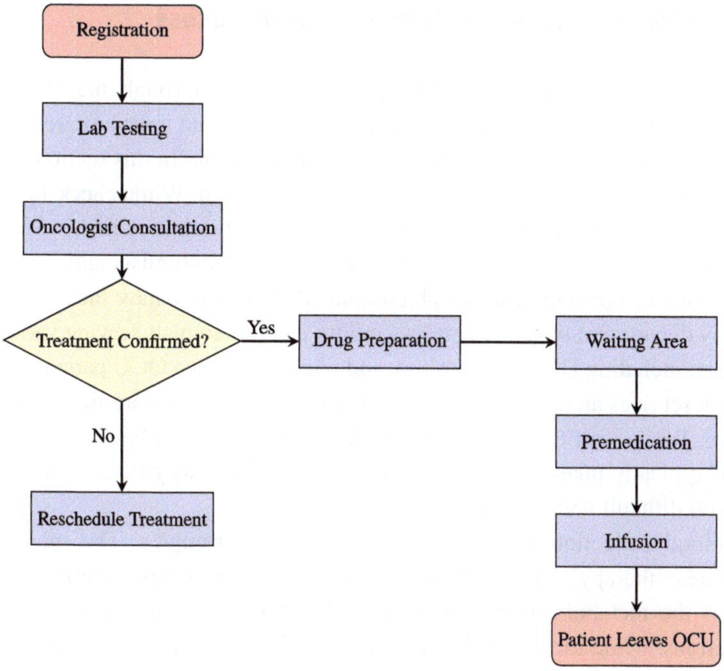

Fig. 1.1 Patient flow in chemotherapy treatment

available, the patient is escorted to a chemotherapy chair to begin the premedication process.

- *Premedication*: The patient is prepared for infusion and given medications, such as anti-nausea drugs and steroids, to help manage potential side effects. During this process, a nurse closely monitors the patient to ensure their safety and comfort.
- *Infusion*: Chemotherapy drugs are administered via intravenous infusion while the patient remains in the same chair. The nurse primarily monitors the infusion to ensure the drug flows correctly, allowing them to oversee multiple patients simultaneously. Once the infusion is complete, the patient leaves the OCU.

Some OCUs may prefer conducting lab tests in the phlebotomy department and/or oncologist consultations the day before treatment. Some divide patients into groups, asking certain groups to visit the phlebotomy department or oncologists a day earlier. When this approach is used, patients must visit the OCU on two consecutive days. For example, van Lent et al. [15] recommended that patients undergoing long treatments have phlebotomy the day before. Although some hospitals separate oncologist consultations and chemotherapy treatments to improve efficiency, Lau et al. [14] found that patients generally prefer having them on the same day due to convenience and transportation challenges.

1.3 Critical Resources in Chemotherapy Process

The primary resources involved in the patient pathway through the OCU, which is discussed in Sect. 1.2 and illustrated in Fig. 1.1, are critical and must be carefully managed to ensure efficient patient flow and maintain staff satisfaction. In this section, we focus on the key resources involved in the steps following registration. While check-in personnel at registration are also important, they are unlikely to be the bottleneck in the overall process.

In the lab testing phase, the critical resources are phlebotomists and lab technicians. During this phase, a patient visits the phlebotomy department to have their blood drawn. A phlebotomy department typically employs multiple phlebotomists serving various hospital departments, including OCU, hematology and oncology. Since OCU patients compete for phlebotomy services alongside patients from other departments, careful coordination may be required. While wait times for an available phlebotomist can be significant, the blood draw itself typically takes around five minutes, though it may extend to ten minutes for patients with difficult vein access.

After blood collection, lab technicians analyze the samples. The most commonly used pre-chemotherapy tests to assess treatment tolerance are the complete blood count (CBC) and the metabolic profile (Chem-7). The CBC evaluates a patient's ability to fight infections, while the Chem-7 assesses organ function, particularly liver and kidney performance. Both tests are typically required for chemotherapy patients, with Chem-7 generally taking longer to process. On average, lab results are available within 75 minutes, but processing times can range from 45 to 150 minutes [20]. During this period, patients must wait in the OCU waiting area.

When the lab results become available, the oncologist consultation begins. In this phase, the oncologist is the primary resource. Since each oncologist tracks the chemotherapy process of a specific set of patients throughout their treatment, a patient only competes with those patients to receive service from their oncologist on a treatment day. The oncologist consultation typically lasts between 15 and 30 minutes [17]. During the consultation, the oncologist reviews key lab results, including white blood cell count, hemoglobin levels, liver and kidney function tests, and electrolyte levels, to assess the patient's health condition. They also discuss any side effects or symptoms the patient may have experienced since the last session, such as nausea and fatigue, and may perform a brief physical examination to check for signs of complications. When necessary, the oncologist consults with other specialists to ensure that the patient's health status is adequate to proceed with treatment. As illustrated in Fig. 1.1, patients who are deemed fit for treatment proceed to the infusion area, while those who are not leave the OCU. The average deferral rate is typically no greater than 20%, based on data from the Odette Cancer Center in Toronto, Ontario, Canada, and the ICL chemotherapy clinic in Saint-Étienne, France [10, 12].

For patients whose treatment is approved, the drug preparation process begins immediately. Chemotherapy drugs are prepared in the hospital pharmacy, which typically employs multiple pharmacists. For example, the OCU at the U.S. Veterans Affairs Medical Center

Table 1.2 Overview of resource use, duration, and key features across chemotherapy treatment steps

Step	Primary resources	Duration	Notable characteristics
Phlebotomy	Phlebotomist	5–10 minutes	Shared with other departments.
Lab testing	Lab Technician	45–150 minutes	Patients wait in the waiting area.
Oncologist consultation	Oncologist	15–30 minutes	Each oncologist has their own set of patients.
Drug preparation	Pharmacist	30–50 minutes	Separate pharmacist roles.
Premedication	Nurse, Chair	15 minutes	Requires full attention of nurse.
Infusion	Nurse (partial), Chair	16–217 minutes	Uses 25% of nurse's capacity per patient; highly variable duration.

in Durham, North Carolina, has a dedicated pharmacy adjacent to the OCU and staffs two pharmacists [20]. One pharmacist is responsible for entering patient and drug order data into the system and printing drug labels, while the other pharmacist organizes all necessary supplies and prepares the drugs in the clean room under a ventilation hood. The whole process takes between 30 and 50 minutes [20].

When the drug is ready, the patient's treatment starts with the premedication step. During this phase, the patient is prepared for infusion and given medications to prevent potential side effects. A chair and a nurse are the primary resources required. The patient needs the full capacity of a nurse during this step, as close monitoring is essential. This phase typically takes around 15 minutes [11].

After premedication, the infusion phase begins. During this stage, a chair and a nurse remain the primary resources required. However, only a fraction of the nurse's capacity is needed—on average, each patient utilizes about one-fourth of a nurse's capacity. The duration of this phase is highly variable; for instance, in the OCU at Hacettepe University Oncology Hospital in Ankara, Turkey, it ranges from 16 to 217 minutes [9].

Table 1.2 provides a summary of the key resources, duration ranges, and distinctive operational characteristics associated with each step in the chemotherapy treatment process.

References

1. Abuzetun, J. Y., et al. (2009) The Stanford V regimen is effective in patients with good risk Hodgkin lymphoma but radiotherapy is a necessary component. *British Journal of Haematology, 144*(4), 531–537.
2. Aggarwal, A., et al. (2024). The future of cancer care in the UK-time for a radical and sustainable National Cancer Plan. In *The Lancet Oncology, 25*(1), e6–e17 (2024)
3. American Cancer Society. (2019). *How is chemotherapy used to treat cancer?* Accessed 29 Jan, 2025. https://www.cancer.org/treatment/treatments-and-side-effects/treatment-types/chemotherapy/how-is-chemotherapy-used-to-treat-cancer.html.

4. American Cancer Society. (2025). *Cancer Facts & Figures*. Accessed 09 Jan, 2026. https://www.cancer.org/research/cancer-facts-statistics/all-cancer-facts-figures/2025-cancer-facts-figures.html.
5. American Cancer Society. (2025). *Getting IV or injectable chemotherapy*. Accessed 17 Feb, 2025. https://www.cancer.org/cancer/managing-cancer/treatment-types/chemotherapy/getting-chemotherapy.html.
6. Bray, F., et al. (2024). Global cancer statistics 2022: GLOBOCAN estimates of incidence and mortality worldwide for 36 cancers in 185 countries. *CA: A Cancer Journal for Clinicians, 74*(3), 229–263.
7. Cancer Research UK. (2025). *Where you have chemotherapy*. Accessed Feb 17, 2025. https://www.cancerresearchuk.org/about-cancer/treatment/chemotherapy/how-you-have/where-you-have.
8. Chang, J. (2000). Chemotherapy dose reduction and delay in clinical practice: Evaluating the risk to patient outcome in adjuvant chemotherapy for breast cancer. *European Journal of Cancer, 36*(Suppl 1), 11–14.
9. Demir, N. B., Gul, S., & Çelik. M. (2021). A stochastic programming approach for chemotherapy appointment scheduling. *Naval Research Logistics, 68*(1), 112–133.
10. Garaix, T., Rostami, S., & Xie, X. (2020). Daily outpatient chemotherapy appointment scheduling with random deferrals. *Flexible Services and Manufacturing Journal, 32*, 129–153.
11. Gul, S. (2024). Nursing care flexibility in chemotherapy appointment scheduling. *Flexible Services and Manufacturing Journal, 36*, 918–945.
12. Hahn-Goldberg, S., et al. (2014) Solving the chemotherapy outpatient scheduling problem with constraint programming. *Journal of Applied Operational Research, 6*(3), 135–144.
13. International Agency for Research on Cancer. (2025). *Cancer fact sheets*. World Health Organization.
14. Lau, P. K. H., Watson, M. J., & Hasani, A. (2014). Patients prefer chemotherapy on the same day as their medical oncology outpatient appointment. *Journal of Oncology Practice, 10*(6), e380–e384.
15. van Lent, W. A. M., Goedbloed, N., & van Harten, W. H. (2009). Improving the efficiency of a chemotherapy day unit: Applying a business approach to oncology. *European Journal of Cancer, 45*(5), 800–806.
16. McBride, A., & Persky, D. (2020). Shifting chemotherapy administration from the in-patient to the outpatient setting improves care and reduces costs. *Presented at ACCC 37th virtual national oncology conference. Sept. 2020*. https://bit.ly/3koAWAr.
17. Ozyuksel, E. D., et al. (2025). Coordinating oncologist appointments with chemotherapy treatments under uncertainty. *Computers & Industrial Engineering, 204*, 111123.
18. Peter, N. (2001). What is cancer chemotherapy? *Acta Oncologica, 40*(2–3), 166–174.
19. Rosenthal D. (2007). Consequences of mucositis-induced treatment breaks and dose reductions on head and neck cancer treatment outcomes. *Journal of Supportive Oncology, 5*(9), 23–31.
20. Slocum, R. F., et al. (2021). Improving chemotherapy infusion operations through the simulation of scheduling heuristics: a case study. *Health Systems, 10*(3), 163–178.

2 Chemotherapy Scheduling

Abstract

Chemotherapy scheduling can be broadly divided into two phases: chemotherapy treatment planning and chemotherapy appointment scheduling (CAS). This chapter reviews both phases by outlining the typical scheduling decisions, commonly used performance measures, key influencing factors, sources of uncertainty, and relevant resources, as well as the modeling and solution approaches adopted in the literature. Particular emphasis is placed on CAS, which is the primary focus of this book.

2.1 Key Challenges: Uncertainty, Care Coordination, Fairness

As discussed in Chap. 1, patient flow in an OCU involves the completion of multiple tasks using shared resources. Uncertainty in these tasks and the need to coordinate diverse resources significantly impact the ability to generate effective schedules. To ensure smooth and patient-centered care, scheduling must balance both patient- and provider-related performance measures. Focusing solely on efficiency, however, can lead to inequities among patients and staff. Therefore, three key factors must be carefully considered when designing OCU schedules: *uncertainty*, *care coordination*, and *fairness*.

In this chapter, we present the typical decisions involved in scheduling chemotherapy operations, along with commonly used performance measures, key influencing factors, sources of uncertainty, considered resources, and the modeling and solution approaches typically used. In the following chapters, we provide detailed discussions of mathematical programming models that incorporate uncertainty in infusion durations, fairness among patients, and care coordination among multiple care providers. Uncertainty is examined in detail in Chap. 3, where we also address care coordination (Sect. 3.2.5). Fairness is the focus of Chap. 4, where we discuss how to quantify it, represent it through mathematical

S. Gul, Ö. Karsu, *Chemotherapy Appointment Scheduling*, Synthesis Lectures on Operations Research and Applications, https://doi.org/10.1007/978-3-032-11552-2_2

functions, and integrate it into mathematical programming models. Care coordination, while highly relevant, is presented as a subsection within Chap. 3 since it represents one of several specific model extensions rather than a central theme of the book.

We categorize chemotherapy scheduling problems into two phases based on the time frame considered. The first is the *chemotherapy treatment planning* phase (i.e., inter-day scheduling), and the second is the *chemotherapy appointment scheduling* phase (i.e., intra-day scheduling). In the planning phase, treatment days are assigned to patients according to the constraints of their prescribed regimens. Once these days are determined, specific appointment times are set during the daily scheduling phase. The next section provides a brief overview of the chemotherapy treatment planning problem, followed by a detailed discussion of chemotherapy appointment scheduling—the primary focus of this book.

2.2 Chemotherapy Treatment Planning

In the chemotherapy planning problem, treatments prescribed in a particular cycle of a patient's chemotherapy regimen (e.g., the Stanford-V regimen shown in Table 1.1) are assigned to specific days within a defined planning horizon. Most studies determine the complete treatment schedule for each new patient in advance by considering the rest periods specified in the regimen. A common approach is to assign the first treatment day using a mathematical programming model or a heuristic method [4, 30]. The subsequent treatment days are then automatically determined based on the selected start day and the required rest periods between treatments. A more flexible approach involves jointly deciding the days of multiple treatments in a cycle [7].

Patients are often constrained to start treatment on or after a minimum start date [18,30], and delays before this date may incur penalties. An alternative approach assigns patients before a maximum allowable wait time, giving preference to earlier dates [4]. A more balanced method involves defining a time window within which each treatment can be scheduled. This window may apply only to the first treatment [2] or to all treatments in the cycle [7]. Furthermore, to promote earlier scheduling within the allowed window, assignments to later days can be penalized [7].

To illustrate one possible approach for assigning treatment days, consider an OCU that operates seven days a week. Suppose Appointment 1 of Patient 1 is scheduled for Wednesday of Week 1. The chemotherapy regimen recommends a rest period of at least 5 days and at most 7 days between consecutive treatments. Therefore, scheduling the next treatment before Monday of Week 2 (i.e., fewer than 5 rest days) or after Wednesday of Week 2 (i.e., more than 7 rest days) would incur significant penalties. The relative severity of early versus late penalties depends on patient-specific clinical factors and oncologist assessment. Moreover, even within the acceptable time window, scheduling the treatment on Monday of Week 2 might be preferred over Tuesday or Wednesday, reflecting a tendency to prioritize earlier dates when clinically feasible.

Although the primary focus of chemotherapy treatment planning is assigning patients to treatment days, additional resource allocation decisions—such as chair assignment [20], bed assignment [21], and nurse assignment [6]—are also considered.

Various modeling approaches have been employed to address the chemotherapy treatment planning problem. These include integer programming (IP) [6, 20], mixed-integer programming (MIP) [21], and stochastic mixed-integer programming, which incorporates uncertainty in infusion durations [7].

Due to the complexity of some models, heuristic methods are often required to obtain feasible solutions within a reasonable time frame [4,21]. To handle both the computational limitations associated with long planning horizons and the dynamic arrival of patient requests, rolling horizon strategies are commonly adopted [6, 30]. In a rolling horizon approach, for example, the planning model is solved on day t for a horizon of T days. The assignments for day t are implemented, and the model is re-solved on day $t + 1$ for the updated set of patients, again over a T-day horizon.

While mathematical programming and heuristic approaches are the most prevalent methods for assigning treatments to specific days, alternative modeling frameworks have also been explored. For example, a Markov Decision Process model has been used to determine the number of treatments to schedule each day, rather than assigning individual treatments to specific dates [10]. This aggregate-level decision support is valuable but does not offer patient-specific scheduling. Future research could address this gap by investigating the use of stochastic dynamic programming models to assign individual patients to treatment days.

The typical performance measures considered in chemotherapy treatment planning models include overtime [18, 30], idle time [18, 30], delays in treatment start [2, 4], deviation from treatment time windows [7, 10], treatment prioritization [2, 4], and the number of treatments scheduled or diverted [2, 10].

2.3 Chemotherapy Appointment Scheduling

We now provide details of chemotherapy appointment scheduling (CAS), the problem that this book specifically focuses on. In CAS, the treatment days for each patient are predetermined, and the key decision involves setting appointment times for those treatments on a given day [8, 30].

2.3.1 Setting Patient Appointment Times

Most studies set appointment times by assigning patients to discrete time slots that indicate their scheduled start times [19,22]. The duration of these time slots is typically 15 minutes, and patients are assumed to occupy consecutive slots based on their treatment durations.

Discretizing the schedule using fixed time slots simplifies planning for OCUs. However, it may also introduce inefficiencies. When treatment durations do not align with slot lengths, idle time can result. For instance, a treatment expected to last 32 minutes would occupy three 15-minute slots, leaving 13 minutes idle in the final slot. Some OCUs adopt even coarser time slots. For example, Hacettepe University Oncology Hospital in Ankara, Türkiye, schedules treatments into two morning slots (8:00 am, 10:30 am) and two afternoon slots (1:00 pm, 3:30 pm), assigning one patient to a chair in each slot [8]. This approach simplifies scheduling but increases potential idle time.

An alternative strategy is employed at the Hospital Clínico de la Red de Salud UC CHRISTUS in Santiago, Chile, where only two slots are defined—8:30 am and 1:30 pm—despite operating from 8:30 am to 8:30 pm [4]. Multiple patients are assigned to each slot, which may reduce idle time but can result in significant patient waiting. Clinics may adopt such coarse slotting schemes to reduce complexity and improve overall system utilization, even at the cost of increased wait times.

While using fixed-length time slots is more common in practice due to ease of implementation, a more efficient approach is to allow appointments at any integer time point. This level of flexibility, however, is typically avoided in real-world settings because it is difficult to implement without the support of a decision tool. Recent studies have adopted models that permit assigning patients to any integer appointment time [5, 28]. From a modeling perspective, both fixed-slot and integer-time formulations are equally complex [28]. Let x_i denote the nonnegative integer appointment time of patient i in a CAS model. A fixed-length slot version can be derived by defining $x_i = \alpha y_i$, where α represents the slot length and y_i is the slot index assigned to patient i. Once the CAS model is solved and y_i is determined, the corresponding appointment time x_i can be obtained using this transformation.

Continuous-time representations of patient appointment times in CAS models have also been adopted in several studies [3, 12, 27]. This modeling approach generally offers advantages in terms of solution times, as it replaces integer variables with continuous ones, thereby reducing computational complexity. However, the resulting appointment times cannot be directly implemented in practice. Post-processing steps, such as rounding heuristics, are typically required to convert continuous solutions into feasible and actionable schedules.

When patients are assigned integer-valued appointment times, solving the CAS model typically involves two steps: first sequencing the patients on the daily treatment list, and then determining their appointment times based on that sequence. Due to the computational complexity of this joint decision-making process, some studies assume that the patient sequence is predetermined and focus solely on assigning appointment times [3, 11]. These models are intended for schedule refinement rather than initial scheduling. In this context, it is assumed that OCU managers have already generated a daily patient schedule, and the model is employed—typically one or two days before the treatment day—to make minor adjustments to appointment times. Despite their limited scope, such refinements can lead to substantial performance improvements in OCUs.

2.3.2 Nurse Assignment

In CAS models, another important decision involves assigning patients to nurses, as nurses are critical resources in the treatment process. While some models consider only aggregate nurse capacity constraints when generating schedules, the majority of studies—including [1, 16, 24]—explicitly determine the nurse assigned to each patient during appointment scheduling.

In many CAS models, nurses are assumed to have identical skills [5, 8, 28]. However, other models—such as those proposed by Liang et al. [24] and Karakaya et al. [22]—account for nurse–patient compatibility, where each nurse is qualified to treat only a specific subset of patients. This subset is typically determined by the acuity level of the patient, which reflects the required intensity of care, and the skill level of the nurse. To ensure high-quality care, several models also restrict the number of patients a nurse can treat simultaneously [22, 24, 30]. A detailed example of such a model is presented in Chap. 3.

In practice, the nature of nurse assignment differs between the premedication and infusion steps. During premedication, a nurse is typically assigned to only one patient at a time, as this step demands close monitoring. In contrast, during the infusion step, a nurse may supervise multiple patients concurrently. All CAS models ensure that a nurse is dedicated to a single patient during the premedication phase. However, nurse assignment during infusion is modeled in varying ways. The most accurate approach is to impose a constraint on the total acuity level of patients simultaneously assigned to a nurse. Nonetheless, some models simplify this by omitting acuity considerations and instead limit the number of concurrent patients per nurse to a maximum of four—reflecting the widely accepted 1:4 nurse–patient ratio in both practice and the literature [4, 8]. Notably, studies incorporating patient acuity have shown that optimal schedules may deviate from this standard ratio [22].

Additional considerations also arise when assigning patients to nurses in CAS models. One such consideration is workload balancing across nurses, which has been addressed in several studies [11, 16, 17]. An example of a CAS model incorporating workload balancing is presented in Chap. 3 of this book. Another important aspect is the flexibility of the nurse–patient assignment system. Some models, such as those by Liang et al. [24] and Gul [12], explore different levels of flexibility. In fully flexible systems, a patient can be assigned to any available nurse with the required skills at each treatment visit, thereby promoting system efficiency. In contrast, inflexible systems require the same nurse to treat a patient across all visits, emphasizing continuity of care. Chapter 3 includes a CAS model that investigates the trade-off between these two approaches.

Furthermore, CAS models may define different categories of nurses to better reflect real-world practices. For example, a patient may have a designated primary nurse and a secondary nurse, with assignments prioritizing the primary nurse when possible [12]. While patients can be assigned to floating nurses—those who are not among the designated primary or secondary nurses—such assignments are generally discouraged, as noted by [20].

The majority of CAS models assume that patient-to-nurse assignment decisions are made in advance, typically at the time patient appointment times are determined [14, 17, 22]. However, some models assume that these decisions are made after the patient arrives at the OCU [5, 8, 28]. Both approaches are observed in practice. When nurses have similar skill levels and are capable of treating any patient, assigning nurses after patient arrival is generally more efficient, as it better accommodates deviations from the schedule caused by uncertainties in treatment durations. For example, suppose there are two nurses, and a patient has been preassigned to Nurse 1. If Nurse 1 is occupied with the premedication phase of another patient's treatment when the assigned patient arrives, the patient must wait—even if Nurse 2, who is available and equally qualified, could begin the treatment. Since the assignment was predetermined, Nurse 2 cannot step in. If the assignment decision were made at the time of patient arrival, this waiting time could be avoided by assigning the patient to the first available nurse.

2.3.3 Chair Assignment

While some CAS models incorporate chairs only as capacity constraints when setting appointment times, several others make explicit patient-to-chair assignments [3, 5, 14].

In chemotherapy treatment processes, chairs are considered identical resources. As a result, specific chair assignments are typically made only after the patient arrives at the OCU. Among the existing models, only a few studies reflect this practice by deferring chair assignments until patient arrival [8, 28]. Aligning the model with this practical approach not only improves realism but also enhances patient flow efficiency, similar to the benefits observed when deferring nurse assignments.

2.3.4 Consideration of Uncertainty

Although earlier modeling efforts often ignored uncertainty in treatment durations, the majority of recent studies explicitly account for it when scheduling appointments [12, 14, 27]. Additionally, some studies have addressed multiple sources of uncertainty by adopting discrete-event simulation (DES) models [25, 26, 29].

Among the various sources of uncertainty in CAS models, infusion duration uncertainty is the most critical and is incorporated in the majority of recent studies [5, 14, 27]. Some models also account for uncertainty in premedication durations [3, 8, 14]. However, other studies argue that the variability in premedication times is relatively low and can be reasonably omitted from the model [5, 28].

Another important source of uncertainty is the treatment approval status, which depends on the oncologist's evaluation conducted on the day of chemotherapy. This uncertainty is explicitly considered in CAS models that focus on the integrated scheduling of oncologist consultations and chemotherapy treatments [9, 14, 28].

While the above three factors are the most commonly considered sources of uncertainty, some CAS models also incorporate additional uncertain elements. For example, Hahn-Goldberg et al. [15] consider uncertainty in the arrival of appointment requests; Mandelbaum et al. [27] account for patient unpunctuality; and Alvarado and Ntaimo [1] include uncertainty in patient acuity levels and the number of nurses available on the treatment day. Among these, patient unpunctuality may significantly impact scheduling outcomes and is worth modeling. However, the uncertainty in the remaining factors may be necessary to consider only in specific cases and can often be omitted to avoid overly complex or unsolvable models.

2.3.5 Performance Measures

When creating chemotherapy appointment schedules, it is essential to consider both patient- and provider-related performance measures simultaneously. Among patient-centered metrics, patient waiting time (i.e., direct waiting time) is a widely accepted proxy for patient satisfaction. It is also the most frequently considered performance measure in CAS models [3, 8, 24].

In models that ignore uncertainty, patient waiting time is typically calculated as the difference between the planned treatment start time and the patient's ready time [16, 24]. However, this representation is limited in capturing the true meaning of wait times. When uncertainty is incorporated—as in Mandelbaum et al. [27] and Karakaya et al. [22]—waiting time instead measures the difference between the actual treatment start time and the scheduled appointment time *in each scenario*. Under a risk-neutral framework, the expected waiting time is obtained by averaging these scenario-based wait times [8, 14]. Alternatively, when robust optimization or risk-averse strategies are employed, different formulations of patient waiting time may be adopted to capture worst-case outcomes or mitigate variability in a more conservative manner [1, 27]. To promote both equity and efficiency, fairness in waiting times across patients is also incorporated as a performance metric [5].

Another commonly used performance measure in CAS models is overtime, typically represented as nurse overtime [8, 17, 24]. Nurse overtime is defined as the amount of time a nurse works beyond their regular shift and is calculated as the difference between the departure time of the last patient treated by the nurse and the scheduled end of the nurse's shift.

In CAS models that account for uncertainty, overtime is computed separately for each scenario. Depending on the risk preference adopted in the model, these scenario-specific values are aggregated using different approaches. For instance, in risk-neutral models, the expected overtime across all scenarios is typically used. In contrast, risk-averse or robust optimization models may rely on alternative formulations, such as worst-case overtime or conditional value-at-risk.

Some CAS models use makespan—also referred to as total working time—as the primary provider-related performance metric [4,28]. Makespan represents the closure time of the OCU, typically defined as the departure time of the last patient. When uncertainty in treatment durations is incorporated, the makespan is computed for each scenario and then aggregated across scenarios to evaluate system performance [9, 28]. The use of makespan can be particularly valuable in CAS models that involve multiple types of human resources, such as oncologists and nurses. In other words, when integrated scheduling of appointments is considered in a multi-stage setting, makespan may be an appropriate measure to account for the departure of the patient from the whole system.

Even though clinic or staff idle time is commonly considered in general outpatient clinic scheduling models, it is explicitly addressed in only a few CAS models, specifically in Demir et al. [8] and Hesaraki et al. [17]. One reason for this is that minimizing overtime often indirectly helps reduce idle time, as also emphasized by Demir et al. [8]. Moreover, appointment times can be manipulated to influence when idle periods are likely to occur during the day. For instance, if appointment start times are minimized in the objective function, appointments will be scheduled earlier in the day, causing idle slots to accumulate toward the end. These later idle periods can then be reserved for contingencies, as suggested in Cataldo et al. [4].

Figure 2.1 illustrates a simplified example designed to clarify the definitions of waiting time, overtime, idle time, and makespan. In this example, four patients are treated by a single nurse using two chairs. Patients 1, 3, and 4 do not experience any waiting, as their treatments begin precisely at their scheduled appointment times (A_i for patient i). Patient 2, however, starts later than their scheduled appointment time and must wait before treatment can begin. First, they wait for the nurse to become available, as the nurse is completing the premedication of Patient 3 and becomes free shortly after Patient 2's arrival. Then, Patient 2 must also wait for a chair to become available. As a result,

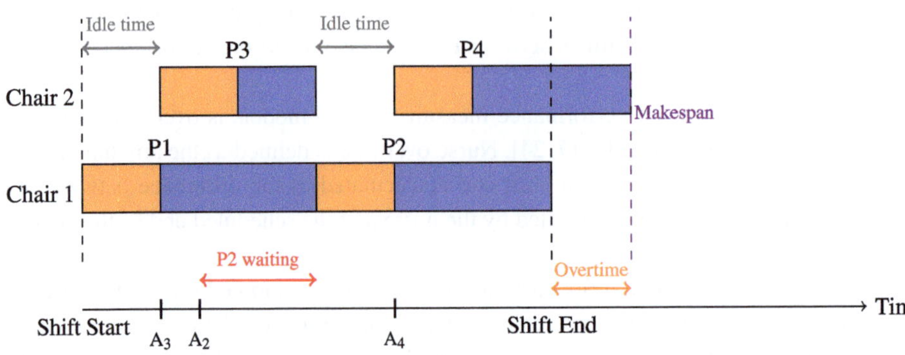

Fig. 2.1 Patient flow over two chairs with appointments (A_i), premedication (*orange*), and infusion (*blue*). Waiting time, nurse overtime, OCU idle time, and makespan are illustrated

their waiting time is extended. The OCU remains idle before Patient 3 starts treatment on Chair 2, as the nurse can only manage one premedication at a time. Therefore, treatment on Chair 2 cannot start until the premedication of the other patient on Chair 1 is completed. A similar idle period occurs before the treatment of Patient 4 begins. The makespan is defined by the departure time of the last patient, which in this case is Patient 4. The difference between this departure time and the end of the scheduled shift corresponds to the nurse overtime.

The performance measures illustrated in Fig. 2.1 are also commonly considered in scheduling models for general outpatient clinics. However, some measures are particularly relevant in the context of CAS models. For example, balancing the instantaneous workload among nurses is addressed in multiple CAS models [1, 22, 24]. This is typically achieved by minimizing excess acuity levels assigned to each nurse. Specifically, the total acuity level of patients assigned to a nurse is calculated and penalized if it exceeds the nurse's capacity. An example of this modeling approach, based on Karakaya et al. [22], is provided in detail in Chap. 3.

Balancing the total daily workload among nurses is another performance measure considered in CAS models [16, 17]. In such models, penalties are incurred when a nurse's workload exceeds the average daily workload. An alternative approach to promoting workload balance is to limit the number of patients assigned to each nurse. This can be modeled as a soft constraint—where deviations from target allocations are penalized in the objective function—as in Benzaid et al. [2], or as a hard constraint, where deviations are strictly prohibited, as in Gul [11]. Workload balance can also be achieved by first grouping patients into categories and then limiting the number of patients from each group assigned to a nurse. An example of this approach, based on Gul [11], is provided in Chap. 3.

Other performance measures are considered in only a few CAS models. For example, during the chemotherapy process, a patient may be monitored by multiple nurses, meaning that nurses may transfer their duties to one another. Such handovers are generally minimized, as fewer changes contribute to safer treatments and reduce confusion for both patients and nurses [16, 17].

Minimizing the number of nurses required during the treatment day is another objective considered in some CAS models [2]. An alternative approach focuses specifically on minimizing assignments to floating nurses, as such assignments are generally not preferred in OCUs. While assigning patients to floating nurses may be necessary during periods of high workload, these assignments should be minimized during the scheduling of chemotherapy treatments [20].

Balancing chair utilization is another performance metric considered in some models. This is typically achieved by minimizing the difference between the maximum and minimum number of chairs in use across time slots [25].

More comprehensive CAS models integrate the scheduling of oncologist consultations and chemotherapy treatments, as a lack of coordination between these steps can lead to significant inefficiencies [9, 14, 28]. Coordinated scheduling may not be necessary if the consultation and drug preparation occur the day before treatment. However, in many OCUs, these steps are performed on the same day to avoid requiring patients to make two separate visits. When same-day coordination is used, some patients may be deemed unfit for treatment during the consultation and asked to reschedule. For those approved, drug preparation begins only after the consultation, resulting in a waiting period before they can proceed to infusion. Therefore, when consultations, drug preparation, and infusion all occur on the same day, it is essential to coordinate these activities to ensure an efficient and patient-centered schedule. In such models, performance measures still include patient waiting time, overtime, and other metrics discussed earlier. However, additional measures related to oncologists and examination room usage may also be considered. For instance, the utilization of oncologist examination rooms can be balanced by minimizing the difference between the maximum and minimum number of rooms used across time slots [25].

2.3.6 Modeling Approach

Deterministic CAS models are typically formulated using either IP [20, 25] or MIP [2, 30]. While constraint programming is less commonly used, it has been explored as an alternative approach [15].

When treatment duration uncertainty is considered, two-stage stochastic mixed-integer programming (SMIP) is the most widely adopted modeling framework [3, 8, 22]. A few examples of such models are detailed in Chap. 3. Robust optimization has been used in only one CAS model to date [27]. However, when both efficiency and equity objectives are jointly considered, these approaches may become insufficient due to the increased model complexity. In such cases, nonlinear stochastic mixed-integer programming models may be required [5].

Additionally, some CAS heuristics have been evaluated using DES models [25, 26, 29], which are also commonly employed to assess different OCU design configurations.

2.3.7 Solution Methods

Since CAS models are often computationally intractable for real-size instances, heuristics are commonly employed to obtain feasible solutions within reasonable time limits [3, 16, 17]. With few exceptions (e.g., Haghi et al. [14]) that utilize sample average approximation, most CAS models based on stochastic programming require decomposition techniques to address computational complexity. Commonly used methods include the progressive hedging algorithm [8] and scenario-bundling-based decomposition [12, 22].

More recently, scenario reduction techniques have been adopted to solve SMIP models more efficiently [5, 28]. These techniques aim to approximate the original scenario set with a smaller, representative subset, enabling the use of commercial solvers that would otherwise struggle with the full-scale model due to the large number of scenarios.

In this chapter, we review CAS models by categorizing them based on five key aspects: the typical decisions involved, the performance measures considered, the sources of uncertainty addressed, the modeling approaches used, and the solution methods employed. For alternative review perspectives, we refer the reader to the works of Lame et al. [23] and Hadid et al. [13].

References

1. Alvarado, M., & Ntaimo, L. (2018). Chemotherapy appointment scheduling under uncertainty using mean-risk stochastic integer programming. *Health Care Management Science, 21*(1), 87–104.
2. Benzaid, M., Lahrichi, N., & Rousseau, L.-M. (2020). Chemotherapy appointment scheduling and daily outpatient-nurse assignment. *Health Care Management Science, 23*, 34–50.
3. Castaing, J., et al. (2016). A stochastic programming approach to reduce patient wait times and overtime in an outpatient infusion center. *IIE Transactions on Healthcare Systems Engineering, 6*(3), 111–125.
4. Cataldo, A., et al. (2023). Multi-stage process for chemotherapy scheduling and effective capacity determination. *International Transactions in Operational Research, 30*(1), 151–180.
5. Çelik, B., Gul, S., & Karsu, Ö. (2025). Maintaining fairness in stochastic chemotherapy scheduling. *Omega, 137*, 103338.
6. Condotta, A., & Shakhlevich, N. V. (2014). Scheduling patient appointments via multilevel template: A case study in chemotherapy. *Operations Research for Health Care, 3*(3), 129–144.
7. Dağıstanlı, G. (2025). Planning and scheduling of chemotherapy operations. Ph.D. Thesis. Ankara, Türkiye: Middle East Technical University.
8. Demir, N. B., Gul, S., & Çelik, M. (2021). A stochastic programming approach for chemotherapy appointment scheduling. *Naval Research Logistics, 68*(1), 112–133.
9. Garaix, T., Rostami, S., & Xie, X. (2020). Daily outpatient chemotherapy appointment scheduling with random deferrals. *Flexible Services and Manufacturing Journal, 32*, 129–153.
10. Gocgun, Y., & Puterman, M. L. (2014). Dynamic scheduling with due dates and time windows: An application to chemotherapy patient appointment booking. *Health Care Management Science, 17*, 60–76.
11. Gul, S. (2021). Chemotherapy appointment scheduling under uncertainty by considering workload balance among nurses. *Pamukkale Üniversitesi Mühendislik Bilimleri Dergisi, 27*(4), 570–578. ISSN: 1300-7009.
12. Gul, S. (2024). Nursing care flexibility in chemotherapy appointment scheduling. *Flexible Services and Manufacturing Journal, 36*, 918–945.
13. Hadid, M., et al. (2022). Operations management of outpatient chemotherapy process: An optimization-oriented comprehensive review. *Operations Research Perspectives, 9*, 100214.
14. Haghi, M., et al. (2023). Integrated consultation and chemotherapy scheduling with stochastic treatment times. *Journal of the Operational Research Society, 74*(9), 2012–2027.
15. Hahn-Goldberg, S., et al. (2014). Solving the chemotherapy outpatient scheduling problem with constraint programming. *Journal of Applied Operational Research, 6*(3), 135–144.
16. Hesaraki, A., Dellaert, N., & de Kok, T. (2020). Integrating nurse assignment in outpatient chemotherapy appointment scheduling. *OR Spectrum, 42*, 1–29.
17. Hesaraki, A., Dellaert, N., & de Kok, T. (2023). Online scheduling using a fixed template: the case of outpatient chemotherapy drug administration. *Health Care Management Science, 26*, 117–137.

18. Heshmat, M., & Eltawil, A. (2018). A new sequential approach for chemotherapy treatment and facility operations planning. *Operations Research for Health Care, 18*, 33–40.
19. Heshmat, M., Nakata, K., & Eltawil, A. (2018). Solving the patient appointment scheduling problem in outpatient chemotherapy clinics using clustering and mathematical programming. *Computers & Industrial Engineering, 124*.
20. Hooshangi-Tabrizi, P., et al. (2020). Improving patient-care services at an oncology clinic using a flexible and adaptive scheduling procedure. *Expert Systems with Applications, 150*, 113267.
21. Issabakhsh, M., Lee, S., & Kang, H. (2021). Scheduling patient appointment in an infusion center: a mixed integer robust optimization approach. *Health Care Management Science, 24*, 117–139.
22. Karakaya, S., Gul, S., & Çelik, M. (2023). Stochastic scheduling of chemotherapy appointments considering patient acuity levels. *European Journal of Operational Research, 305*(2), 902–916.
23. Lamè, G., Jouini, O., & Cardinal, J. S.-L. (2016). Outpatient chemotherapy planning: A literature review with insights from a case study. *IIE Transactions on Healthcare Systems Engineering, 6*(3), 127–139.
24. Liang, B., & Turkcan, A. (2016). Acuity-based nurse assignment and patient scheduling in oncology clinics. *Health Care Management Science, 19*, 207–226.
25. Liang, B., et al. (2015). Improvement of chemotherapy patient flow and scheduling in an outpatient oncology clinic. *International Journal of Production Research, 53*(24), 7177–7190.
26. Liu, E., et al. (2019). Improving access to chemotherapy through enhanced capacity planning and patient scheduling. *IISE Transactions on Healthcare Systems Engineering, 9*(1), 1–13.
27. Mandelbaum, A., et al. (2020). Data-driven appointment-scheduling under uncertainty: The case of an infusion unit in a cancer center. *Management Science, 66*(1), 243–270.
28. Ozyuksel, E. D., et al. (2025). Coordinating oncologist appointments with chemotherapy treatments under uncertainty. *Computers & Industrial Engineering, 204*, 111123.
29. Slocum, R. F., et al. (2021). Improving chemotherapy infusion operations through the simulation of scheduling heuristics: A case study. *Health Systems, 10*(3), 163–178.
30. Turkcan, A., Zeng, B., & Lawley, M. (2012). Chemotherapy operations planning and scheduling. *IIE Transactions on Healthcare Systems Engineering, 2*(1), 31–49.

Uncertainty in Chemotherapy Scheduling

3

Abstract

Uncertainty in treatment durations is a critical factor in chemotherapy appointment scheduling (CAS). We first examine the sources of variability in treatment times and illustrate their scope using real data from an Outpatient Chemotherapy Unit (OCU). Building on this motivation, we present several two-stage stochastic mixed-integer programming (SMIP) formulations adapted from the literature. We begin with a base model that balances expected patient waiting time and nurse overtime. Recognizing its limitations, we then introduce successive extensions that incorporate daily nurse workload balancing, manage instantaneous nurse workload through acuity-based measures, allow for varying levels of nursing care flexibility, and coordinate oncologist consultations with chemotherapy appointments.

3.1 Scope and Sources of Uncertainty

Several studies in the literature report uncertainty in chemotherapy treatment durations [1, 3]. Uncertainty in the actual length of chemotherapy appointments can significantly impact schedule adherence and resource utilization in chemotherapy clinics. Common sources of variability in chemotherapy durations include:

- *Early Termination of Infusion:* Some patients may not tolerate the treatment well, leading to the premature discontinuation of their infusion.
- *Adverse Reactions and Complications:* Unexpected patient responses, such as allergic or infusion-related reactions, may require interventions that prolong the infusion durations.

S. Gul, Ö. Karsu, *Chemotherapy Appointment Scheduling*, Synthesis Lectures on Operations Research and Applications, https://doi.org/10.1007/978-3-032-11552-2_3

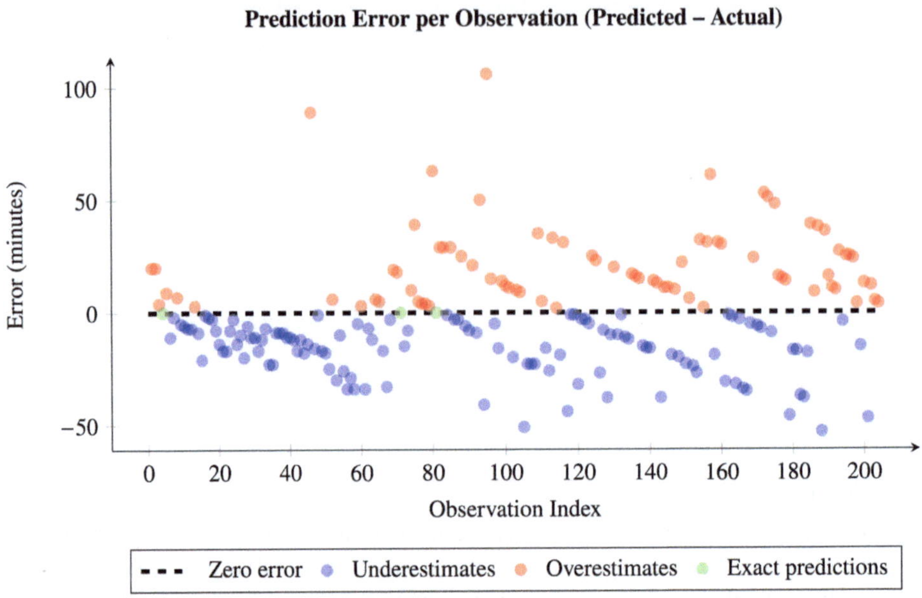

Fig. 3.1 Prediction errors for 204 patients. The x-axis represents patients ordered by their actual treatment durations, while the y-axis shows the difference between predicted and actual values

- *Last-Minute Drug Changes:* Adjustments to the prescribed drug regimen—due to changes in clinical assessment or drug availability—can alter infusion durations from what was originally planned.

The data we collected from an OCU at a major oncology hospital in Ankara, Turkey, illustrates the extent of uncertainty in treatment durations. Figure 3.1 displays the differences between predicted and actual treatment durations for 204 patients. The treatments are ordered by increasing actual duration on the x-axis. As shown, shorter treatments were generally underestimated, while longer treatments exhibited both underestimation and overestimation. Overall, 59% of treatment durations were underestimated, and 41% were overestimated.

The approximately linear trend observed in the deviations—particularly visible among blue points between observations 120 and 160—reflects the discrete set of duration values used for predictions (e.g., 120, 135, or 150 minutes). In other words, the head nurse selects from a limited set of possible durations when estimating treatment times. The durations of only three treatments are estimated with precision. The mean absolute percent error (MAPE) associated with the data set is 16.9% [3]. Given this significant variability, OCU managers must account for uncertainty in treatment durations when scheduling appointments.

Treatment durations range from 16 to 240 minutes. The average premedication duration is 15.3 minutes, while the average infusion duration is 112.5 minutes. The variability in premedication durations is limited, as indicated by a 95% confidence interval of [14.61, 16.09] minutes. Consequently, several recent studies that consider uncertainty in treatment durations assume the premedication duration to be constant [2, 5, 7, 9]. In contrast, uncertainty in infusion durations is carefully addressed in these studies.

3.2 Modeling Chemotherapy Scheduling Problem Under Uncertainty

3.2.1 Base Model

The first model developed in the literature to generate a complete daily schedule for an OCU under uncertainty in treatment durations is that of Demir et al. [3]. While Castaing et al. [1] also addressed a stochastic chemotherapy scheduling problem, their approach assumed a pre-existing schedule and made only minor adjustments by retaining the original patient sequence and revising only the appointment times. Moreover, their model focused on a single nurse and did not account for patient-to-nurse assignments. Therefore, we present a two-stage stochastic mixed-integer programming model adapted from Demir et al. [3]. We simplify their model by excluding uncertainty in premedication durations, as the dataset exhibits a narrow confidence interval for these values. In addition, we omit chair idle time minimization since Demir et al. [3] shows that overtime and idle time are not conflicting objectives in their experiments. The notation used for sets, parameters, and decision variables for the model that we refer to as SMIP-1 is summarized in Table 3.1.

In SMIP-1, a number of assumptions are made:

(i) Patients are assumed to arrive exactly at their scheduled appointment times; thus, appointment time equals arrival time.
(ii) Patients are not assigned to fixed-length time slots, as doing so may result in unnecessary idle time. Appointment times can be set to any integer value.
(iii) Nurses are assumed to have identical skill levels.
(iv) Any patient can be assigned to any available nurse.
(v) The patient arrival sequence is determined by the model and remains fixed throughout the patient's flow in the OCU. This assumption enables an optimal myopic second-stage decision structure, where nurse and chair assignments, as well as treatment start times, are determined for each scenario—thereby justifying the use of a two-stage stochastic programming approach for an inherently dynamic problem.

$$min \quad Q(\mathbf{a}, \mathbf{b}) \tag{3.1}$$

$$s.t. \quad b_{ij} + b_{ji} = 1 \qquad \forall i, j \in I, j > i \tag{3.2}$$

$$a_j \geq a_i - M(1 - b_{ij}) \qquad \forall i, j \in I, j \neq i \tag{3.3}$$

Table 3.1 SMIP-1 model notation

Index sets	
I	Patients
C	Chairs
Ω	Scenarios
N	Nurses
Parameters	
s_i	Premedication duration of patient $i \in I$
t_i^{ω}	Infusion duration of patient $i \in I$ in scenario $\omega \in \Omega$
H	Shift length of nurses
L	Upper limit on nurse overtime
λ	Weight of the waiting time in the interval [0, 1]
M	A large value
First-stage decision variables	
b_{ij}	$= \begin{cases} 1, & \text{if patient } i \in I \text{ precedes patient } j \in I \\ 0, & \text{otherwise} \end{cases}$
a_i	Appointment time for patient $i \in I$
Second-stage decision variables	
x_{in}^{ω}	$= \begin{cases} 1, & \text{if patient } i \in I \text{ is assigned to nurse } n \in N \text{ under scenario } \omega \in \Omega \\ 0, & \text{otherwise} \end{cases}$
y_{ic}^{ω}	$= \begin{cases} 1, & \text{if patient } i \in I \text{ is assigned to chair } c \in C \text{ under scenario } \omega \in \Omega \\ 0, & \text{otherwise} \end{cases}$
w_i^{ω}	Waiting time of patient $i \in I$ under scenario $\omega \in \Omega$
d_i^{ω}	Discharge time of patient $i \in I$ under scenario $\omega \in \Omega$
O_n^{ω}	Overtime for nurse $n \in N$ under scenario $\omega \in \Omega$

$$b_{ij} \in \{0, 1\} \qquad \forall i, j \in I, j \neq i \tag{3.4}$$

$$a_i : integer \qquad \forall i \in I \tag{3.5}$$

where

$\mathcal{Q}(\mathbf{a}, \mathbf{b}) = E_{\xi}[\mathrm{Q}(\mathbf{a}, \mathbf{b}, \xi(\omega))]$is the expected recourse function, and

$$\mathrm{Q}(\mathbf{a}, \mathbf{b}, \xi(\omega)) = \min\left\{\lambda \sum_{i \in I} w_i^{\omega} + (1 - \lambda) \sum_{n \in N} O_n^{\omega}\right\} \tag{3.6}$$

$$s.t. \sum_{n \in N} x_{in}^{\omega} = 1 \qquad \forall i \in I \tag{3.7}$$

$$\sum_{c \in C} y_{ic}^{\omega} = 1 \qquad \forall i \in I \qquad (3.8)$$

$$a_i + w_i^{\omega} + s_i + t_i^{\omega} = d_i^{\omega} \qquad \forall i \in I \qquad (3.9)$$

$$a_j + w_j^{\omega} \geq a_i + w_i^{\omega} + s_i - M(3 - b_{ij} - x_{in}^{\omega} - x_{jn}^{\omega}) \qquad \forall i, j \in I, j \neq i, \forall n \in N \qquad (3.10)$$

$$a_j + w_j^{\omega} \geq d_i^{\omega} - M(3 - b_{ij} - y_{ic}^{\omega} - y_{jc}^{\omega}) \qquad \forall i, j \in I, j \neq i, \forall c \in C \qquad (3.11)$$

$$a_j + w_j^{\omega} \geq a_i + w_i^{\omega} - M(1 - b_{ij}) \qquad \forall i, j \in I, j \neq i \qquad (3.12)$$

$$O_n^{\omega} \geq d_i^{\omega} - H - M(1 - x_{in}^{\omega}) \qquad \forall i \in I, \forall n \in N \qquad (3.13)$$

$$O_n^{\omega} \leq L \qquad \forall n \in N \qquad (3.14)$$

$$x_{in}^{\omega} \in \{0, 1\} \qquad \forall i \in I, \forall n \in N \qquad (3.15)$$

$$y_{ic}^{\omega} \in \{0, 1\} \qquad \forall i \in I, \forall c \in C \qquad (3.16)$$

$$d_i^{\omega}, w_i^{\omega} \geq 0 \qquad \forall i \in I \qquad (3.17)$$

$$O_n^{\omega} \geq 0 \qquad \forall n \in N \qquad (3.18)$$

The objective function (3.1) minimizes the expected second-stage cost, representing an expected weighted sum of total patient waiting time and total nurse overtime. Constraints (3.2) define the daily patient sequence by establishing precedence relationships. Constraints (3.3) ensure that appointment times are consistent with this sequence. Constraints (3.4)–(3.5) impose binary and integrality restrictions on the first-stage variables.

The second-stage objective function (3.6) minimizes the scenario-dependent cost for each $\omega \in \Omega$, specifically the weighted sum of total patient waiting time and nurse overtime. Constraints (3.7) and (3.8) assign each patient to exactly one nurse and one chair, respectively. Constraints (3.9) compute each patient's discharge time by summing their appointment time, waiting time, premedication duration, and infusion duration.

Constraints (3.10) regulate the treatment sequence for patients assigned to the same nurse. A patient's treatment can only begin after the previous patient's premedication ends, since nurses cannot manage multiple premedications simultaneously due to the need for close supervision during this phase. Similarly, constraints (3.11) ensure that patients sharing a chair are treated sequentially, as only one patient can occupy a chair at a time.

Constraints (3.12) ensure that the actual treatment start order aligns with the patient arrival sequence, in accordance with Assumption (v). Specifically, when a nurse and a chair become available, they are assigned to the earliest arriving patient among those waiting, allowing treatment to start without delay. This assignment rule, which we refer to as *Policy 1*, is shown to be optimal in the context of the SMIP-1 model by [3].

Constraints (3.13) compute the overtime for each nurse, while constraints (3.14) limit it from above. Finally, constraints (3.15)–(3.18) define binary and nonnegativity restrictions for second-stage variables.

SMIP-1 solutions yield valuable schedules for OCUs by addressing fundamental aspects of chemotherapy appointment scheduling and balancing the trade-off between patient and provider satisfaction. However, despite its strengths, SMIP-1 overlooks several practically relevant features and may not be suitable for all OCU environments.

The key limitations of the SMIP-1 model are as follows:

- Nurse workload balance: It does not incorporate explicit mechanisms to balance the total daily workload among nurses, potentially resulting in uneven nurse utilization. Workload balance is only indirectly addressed by excluding schedules in which a single nurse incurs excessive overtime, as imposed by constraints (3.14). However, this approach does not ensure true workload balance, since it disregards the complexity of the cases assigned to each nurse.
- Instantaneous nurse workload: It does not enforce any upper bound on the number of patients a nurse may serve at the same time, which can lead to temporary overloads and a potential decline in care quality.
- Pre-approved treatment assumption: It assumes that all patients have already visited their oncologists and received approval for chemotherapy on the previous day, which may not reflect real-world processes in certain OCUs.
- Fairness considerations: While the model promotes efficiency through the performance measures used in the objective function, it does not explicitly address fairness among patients.

In the following sections, we address each of these limitations in detail and propose enhancements to the SMIP-1 model to improve its applicability and robustness in real-world OCU operations.

3.2.2 Nurse Workload Balance

Some patients in the OCU may require more intensive nursing attention during chemotherapy. Consequently, even if two nurses are assigned the same number of patients, their total workloads may be unbalanced if one cares for significantly more complex cases.

Table 3.2 Additional notation for SMIP-2

Additional sets and parameters	
K	Set of patient classes
I_k	Set of patients in class k
P_k	Maximum number of patients from class k that can be assigned to a nurse

To address this, various modeling approaches can be used to incorporate workload balancing constraints. For example, Gul [4] categorize patients into classes based on their nursing care requirements and impose daily limits on the number of patients from each class that a nurse can serve. Let SMIP-2 denote the extension of SMIP-1 that incorporates a nurse workload balancing constraint. Table 3.2 presents the additional sets and parameters introduced for this extension. The corresponding constraints are represented by constraints (3.19).

$$\sum_{i \in I_k} x_{in}^{\omega} \le P_k \quad \forall n \in N, \forall k \in K \tag{3.19}$$

Note that introducing constraints (3.19) disrupts the favorable structure of the SMIP-1 model, which admits an optimal myopic nurse and chair assignment policy—Policy 1—where the earliest arriving patient is assigned to the first available nurse and chair. Under the revised model, this policy no longer guarantees optimality in the second-stage subproblems, as the workload balancing constraint across patient classes introduces coupling between assignment decisions.

The inclusion of constraints (3.19) necessitates solving an optimization problem each time a nurse or a chair becomes available. However, this approach is neither practical nor implementable in real-time clinical settings. To overcome this limitation, nurse and chair assignment decisions must be shifted to the first stage. Accordingly, the second-stage scenario-dependent decision variables x_{in}^{ω} and y_{ic}^{ω} are replaced with scenario-independent variables x_{in} and y_{ic}, respectively, in the SMIP-2 model. The updated versions of constraints (3.7), (3.8), and (3.19) are included in the first stage of SMIP-2, as they involve only first-stage decision variables following this revision.

3.2.3 Instantaneous Nurse Workload

Even though SMIP-2 ensures a balanced total daily workload among nurses, it does not prevent excessive workload at specific moments during the day. This is because a nurse may simultaneously monitor multiple patients receiving infusions. If the number of patients under a nurse's supervision exceeds their capacity at any given time, the quality of care may decline, and the risk of nurse fatigue may increase significantly. To address this issue, Karakaya et al. [7] extend the work of Demir et al. [3] by incorporating constraints

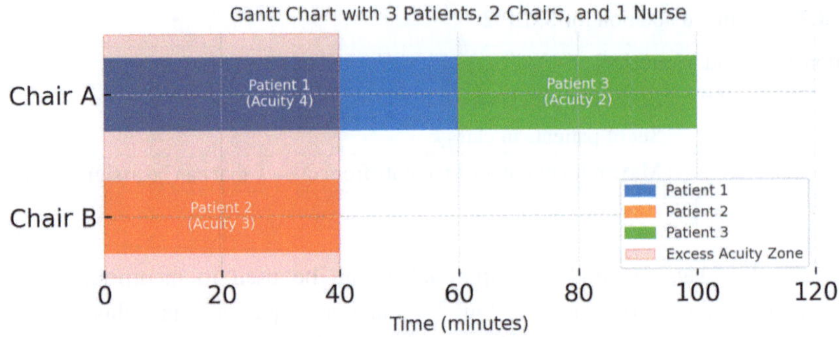

Fig. 3.2 Gantt chart with 3 patients receiving care on 2 chairs by a single nurse. The shaded region indicates a time interval where the combined acuity of simultaneously treated patients exceeds the recommended nurse workload threshold

that consider nurses' instantaneous workload. In their approach, the intensity of nursing care required by a patient is quantified using patient acuity. Each nurse has a skill level that limits them to treating patients with acuity levels not exceeding a specific threshold. Moreover, a nurse's instantaneous workload is defined as the sum of the acuity levels of all patients they are attending to simultaneously. When this total exceeds the nurse's capacity, the excess acuity is penalized in the objective function to discourage overload. Accordingly, their model minimizes the total excess acuity above the target workload to balance nurses' instantaneous workloads.

For example, in Fig. 3.2, Patients 1 and 2 are treated simultaneously by the same nurse on two different chairs. The nurse is qualified to care for patients with acuity levels up to 4 individually. Patient 1 has an acuity level of 4, and Patient 2 has a level of 3. While the nurse is capable of treating each patient independently, providing care to both at the same time results in a combined acuity of 7, which exceeds the desirable total acuity threshold of 5 by 2 units. To discourage such overloads, Karakaya et al. [7] introduce a scheduling approach that penalizes the expected value of these excess acuity levels. Had Patient 3, with a lower acuity level, been scheduled before Patient 1, the total instantaneous workload would have remained within the preferred limit.

Let SMIP-3 represent the model that minimizes expected excess acuity over the nurses' capacities. As in SMIP-2, nurse and chair assignment decisions must be made in the first stage of the SMIP-3 due to the same reasons discussed in Sect. 3.2.2. Since the instantenous workload needs to be checked at a given moment, the whole scheduling period within a day must be discretized and divided into time slots for modeling purposes. Table 3.3 presents the additional parameters and sets introduced for this purpose in addition to the ones of SMIP-1 and SMIP-2.

The constraint to be added to the first stage is as follows:

$$\sum_{s \in S} t_{is} = 1 \quad \forall i \in I \tag{3.20}$$

Table 3.3 Additional notation for SMIP-3

Additional sets, parameters and decision variables	
θ_i	Acuity level of patient $i \in I$
I_n	Set of patients who can be assigned to nurse $n \in N$, based on skill compatibility
S	Set of time slots
q_s	Beginning time of slot $s \in S$
t_{is}	$= \begin{cases} 1, & \text{if patient } i \in I \text{ is assigned to time slot } s \in S \\ 0, & \text{otherwise} \end{cases}$
z_{ins}^{ω}	$= \begin{cases} 1, & \text{if the treatment of patient } i \in I \text{ starts at slot } s \in S \text{ by nurse } n \in N \text{ under scenario } \omega \in \Omega \\ 0, & \text{otherwise} \end{cases}$
e_n^{ω}	Excess acuity over the capacity of the nurse $n \in N$ under scenario $\omega \in \Omega$
m_n	Desired capacity threshold of nurse $n \in N$ in terms of acuity
f_{is}^{ω}	Earliest time slot at which the treatment of patient $i \in I$ must have started, given that the treatment is ongoing at slot $s \in S$ under scenario $\omega \in \Omega$

Constraint (3.20) ensures that each patient is assigned to a slot within the day. Constraint (3.3) in SMIP-1 is also revised in SMIP-3 to ensure that the appointment times are represented in terms of slots. Specifically, a_i in constraint (3.3) is replaced by $\sum_{s \in S} q_s \cdot t_{is}$.

Some differences also arise in the second stage of the model, as actual treatment start times are represented using discrete time slots in SMIP-3. Specifically, the variable z_{ins}^{ω} indicates whether the treatment of patient $i \in I$ is started by nurse $n \in N$ at time slot $s \in S$. To ensure consistency between stages, constraints must enforce that the nurse assigned to a patient in the first stage is also responsible for that patient in the second stage. While the remaining constraints serve similar purposes as those in SMIP-1, they must be adapted to a slot-based structure.

Here, we focus on a constraint unique to SMIP-3, which controls the instantaneous nursing workload—a feature not included in SMIP-1. To formulate this constraint, we identify the patients whose treatments are ongoing at each time slot s, and compute the total acuity level assigned to each nurse. This allows us to detect any excess acuity beyond the nurse's capacity. The corresponding constraint is:

$$\sum_{i \in I_n} \sum_{u=f_{is}^{\omega}}^{s} \theta_i z_{ins}^{\omega} \leq m_n + e_n^{\omega} \quad \forall n \in N, \forall s \in S \tag{3.21}$$

Constraint (3.21) considers patients $i \in I_n$ who can be treated by nurse $n \in N$ based on the nurse's skill level. Among these, it identifies the patients assigned to nurse n whose treatment spans time slot s. The total acuity of such patients is then calculated. If this total exceeds nurse n's desired acuity threshold m_n, the excess is captured by the variable e_n^{ω}, which becomes positive; otherwise, it remains zero.

In SMIP-3, the objective function of the second-stage subproblem (3.6) from SMIP-1 is revised by incorporating an additional term that penalizes excess acuity, specifically $\sum_{n \in N} e_n^{\omega}$ weighted by its corresponding penalty parameter.

3.2.4 Nursing Care Flexibility

In the previous models, it is assumed that a patient can be assigned to any available nurse at a given treatment visit, provided the nurse has the appropriate skill level to administer the treatment. For instance, if five nurses are qualified to treat a patient, the patient can be assigned to any of them, regardless of which nurse treated them in previous chemotherapy sessions. This approach is known as *functional care delivery*, and it represents a *fully flexible system* [8]. Implementing such a system typically results in the most efficient chemotherapy schedules. However, it offers the *lowest level of care continuity*, which may negatively impact the patient experience.

At the opposite end of the spectrum is the *primary care delivery approach*, which prioritizes care continuity. In this model, a patient is always treated by the same nurse throughout their all treatment visits. While this improves the therapeutic relationship between the patient and nurse, and can enhance overall care quality, it significantly limits scheduling flexibility. As a result, primary care delivery often leads to *less efficient schedules*, since the range of feasible appointment times for each patient becomes much narrower.

A survey conducted by the Oncology Nursing Society found that 40% of clinics implement a functional care delivery model, 39% adopt primary care delivery, and the remaining clinics utilize a hybrid approach that balances care continuity and system efficiency [6]. Gul [5] investigates this trade-off by introducing a *partially flexible system*, which is compared against both functional and primary care delivery models.

In the partially flexible system, each patient is assigned a designated *primary nurse*, and the OCU coordinator prioritizes scheduling the patient with this nurse. However, when necessary, patients may also be assigned to other qualified nurses—referred to as *secondary nurses*. Figure 3.3 provides a visual comparison of the three care delivery systems: functional care delivery, partially flexible system, and primary care delivery.

To maintain a balance between flexibility and continuity, the OCU imposes a limit on the total number of assignments made to secondary nurses in the partially flexible systems. This limit, denoted by J, serves as a *control parameter* for system flexibility. If $J = 0$, the OCU enforces a pure primary care delivery model, ensuring each patient is always treated by their primary nurse. Conversely, if J is greater than or equal to the number of patients, the system behaves like a fully flexible functional care model. Intermediate

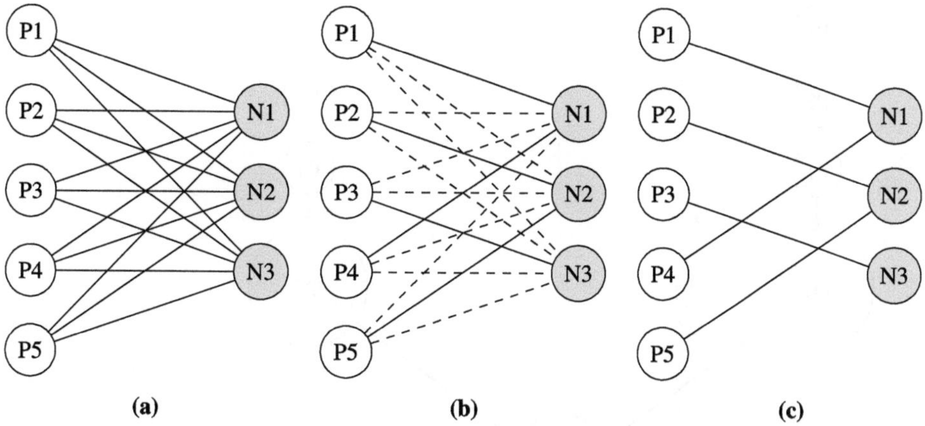

Fig. 3.3 Comparison of care delivery systems. *Dashed lines* in the partially flexible system indicate assignments to secondary nurses. (**a**) Functional care delivery. (**b**) Partially flexible system. (**c**) Primary care delivery

values of J lead to the partially flexible system, where limited deviations from primary nurse assignments are allowed.

We refer to this extension as SMIP-4. In SMIP-4, patient-to-nurse assignments are made in the first stage, as in SMIP-2 and SMIP-3, and are represented by the binary decision variables x_{in}. Let f_{in} be a binary parameter that equals 1 if nurse n is the designated *primary nurse* of patient i, and 0 otherwise. The total number of assignments to secondary nurses is limited using the following constraint:

$$\sum_{n \in N} \sum_{i \in I_n} (1 - f_{in}) x_{in} \leq J \tag{3.22}$$

3.2.5 Coordinating Oncologist Consultation Appointments with Chemotherapy Treatment Appointments

In the previous models, patients are scheduled only for their chemotherapy appointments. This approach is applicable when oncologist consultations are conducted a day prior to treatment. However, in many OCUs, patients undergo oncologist evaluations on the same day as their chemotherapy sessions. In such settings, lack of coordination between the oncologist consultation and chemotherapy treatment can lead to inefficiencies. Moreover, some patients may not be cleared for treatment after the consultation and are asked to reschedule. For those approved, chemotherapy drug preparation must follow, during which patients wait until their medications are ready before being taken to an infusion chair. Therefore, when these steps occur on the same day, it is essential to coordinate

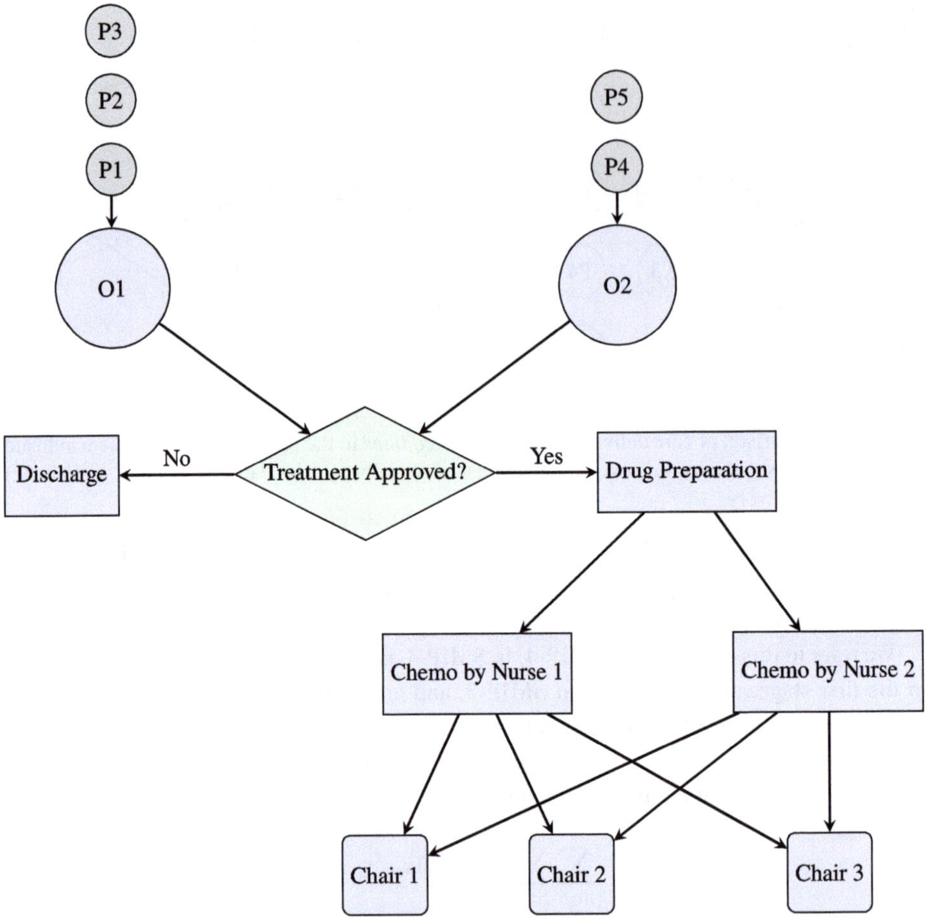

Fig. 3.4 Coordinated patient flow in an OCU where two oncologists conduct consultations, followed by drug preparation and chemotherapy treatment administered by two nurses using three chairs

all activities—consultation, drug preparation, and infusion—to ensure an efficient and patient-centered schedule (see Fig. 3.4).

Furthermore, uncertainty in oncologist treatment approval must be carefully considered. To illustrate its impact on schedule performance, consider the example in Fig. 3.5. Two patients are each seen by a different oncologist, and a single chemotherapy chair becomes available at $t = 80$. Three scenarios are shown. In Fig. 3.5a, both consultations finish at $t = 80$. Patient 1's chemotherapy treatment is not approved and leaves the OCU, so Patient 2 starts treatment immediately (waiting time 0). In Fig. 3.5b, both consultations again finish at $t = 80$. In this case, Patient 1's chemotherapy treatment is approved. With only one chair, Patient 1 is seated first, and Patient 2 waits until Patient 1's treatment ends (about 35–40 minutes). Finally, Fig. 3.5c highlights utilization effects: Only Patient

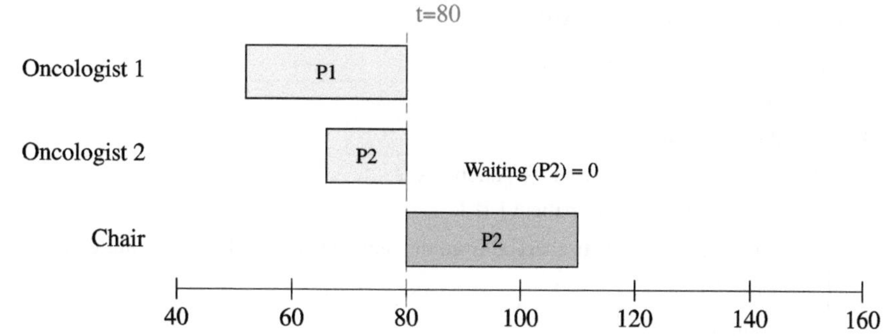

(a) P1 not approved (P2 has zero waiting).

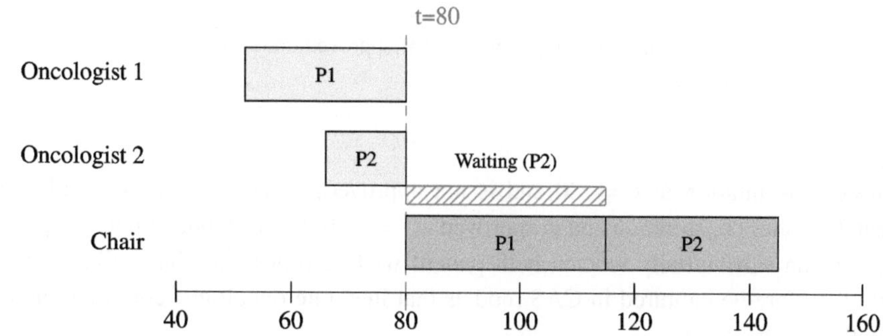

(b) P1 approved (P2 waits positively).

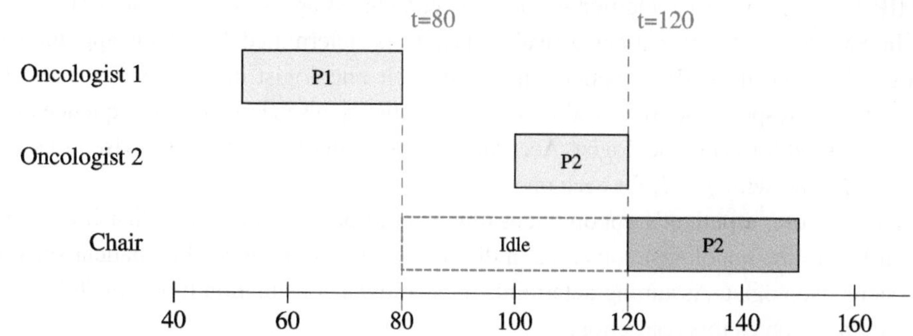

(c) Only P1 ready at $t = 80$; P2 ready at $t = 120$. P1 not approved $\Rightarrow$ chair idle until $t = 120$.

Fig. 3.5 Two oncologists and a single chemotherapy chair with approval uncertainty. Chair is available at t=80. (**a**) Chemotherapy of Patient 1 is not approved: Patient 2 starts immediately (waiting = 0). (**b**) Chemotherapy of Patient 1 is approved: Patient 2 waits until Patient 1's treatment ends. (**c**) Only Patient 1 is ready at t=80 and not approved; Patient 2 becomes ready at t=120, so the chair is idle from t=80 to t=120

Table 3.4 Additional notation for SMIP-5

Additional sets, parameters and variables	
Θ	Oncologists
I_θ	Patients of oncologist $\theta \in \Theta$
o_i	Oncologist consultation duration for patient $i \in I$
k_i	Drug preparation duration for patient $i \in I$
e_{ij}	$= \begin{cases} 1, & \text{if patient } i \in I \text{ is discharged from the oncologist consultation earlier than patient } j \in I \\ 0, & \text{otherwise} \end{cases}$
β_i^ω	$= \begin{cases} 1, & \text{if the treatment of patient } i \in I \text{ is approved under scenario } \omega \in \Omega \\ 0, & \text{otherwise} \end{cases}$
f_i^ω	$= \begin{cases} 1, & \text{Treatment start time of patient } i \in I \text{ if approved under scenario } \omega \in \Omega \\ 0, & \text{otherwise} \end{cases}$

1 finishes consultation at $t = 80$ and is not approved, so the chair remains idle until Patient 2 finishes consultation and is approved at $t = 120$. In short, uncertainty in approval decisions can substantially worsen both patient waiting times and chair utilization, and should therefore be captured in CAS models that integrate oncologist consultations with chemotherapy treatments.

The resulting model, SMIP-5, adapted from the approach of Ozyuksel et al. [9], extends SMIP-1 by incorporating additional variables, parameters and sets (see Table 3.4).

In SMIP-1, a single patient arrival sequence is determined based on appointment times. However, in SMIP-5, patients first visit their oncologist upon arrival. Since each oncologist is responsible for a distinct subset of patients, a separate arrival sequence must be established for each oncologist. Accordingly, constraint (3.2) must be revised to apply to all $i, j \in I_\theta$, with $j \geq i$, for each oncologist $\theta \in \Theta$.

Furthermore, a patient's appointment time should be scheduled such that it does not occur before the oncologist consultation discharge time of any preceding patient seen by the same oncologist. Assuming deterministic oncologist consultation times, the following constraint enforces this restriction:

$$a_j \geq a_i + o_i - M(1 - b_{ij}) \quad \forall i, j \in I_\theta, j \neq i, \forall \theta \in \Theta \tag{3.23}$$

Constraint (3.23) ensures that if patient i precedes patient j in the consultation sequence of oncologist θ, then the appointment time of patient j must be no earlier than the consultation discharge time of patient i.

In SMIP-1, due to assumption (v) and constraint (3.12), the chronological order of patient appointment times and actual chemotherapy start times are aligned. In other words, when multiple patients are awaiting assignment to a chair and a nurse in the OCU, priority is given to the patient who arrived earlier (Policy 1). However, in SMIP-5, this

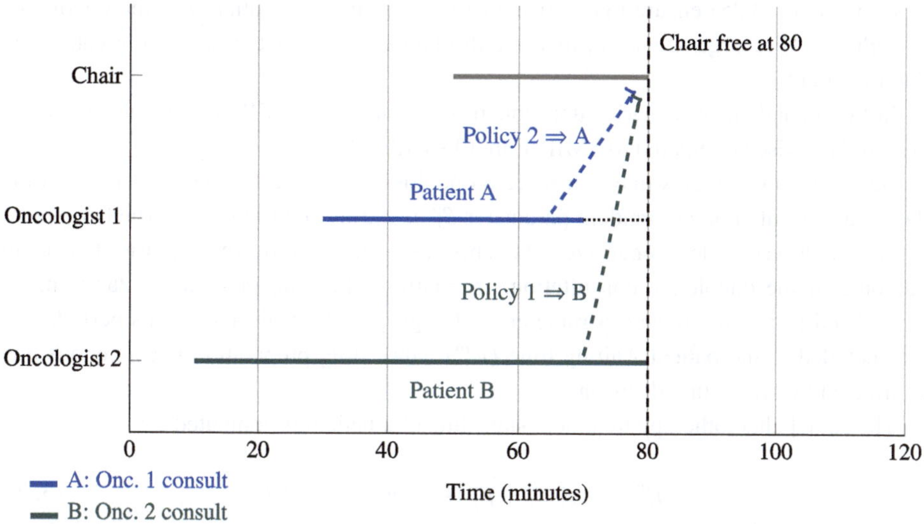

Fig. 3.6 Snapshot illustrating both Policy 1 and Policy 2. When the chair is free, Policy 1 assigns the patient with the earlier arrival (patient B), whereas Policy 2 assigns the patient with the earlier consultation discharge (patient A)

assumption must be revised since patients first undergo an oncologist consultation prior to chemotherapy. As consultation durations vary across patients, priority for chair and nurse assignments should now be based on the time patients are discharged from the oncologist. We refer to this policy as *Policy 2*.

Figure 3.6 compares these policies. Patient A is seen by Oncologist 1, and Patient B by Oncologist 2. Suppose a chair becomes available at time 80, and a nurse is also available to start premedication. Both patients are done with the consultation and ready for assignment at that time. Under Policy 1, Patient B would be assigned because their oncologist appointment started earlier. Under Policy 2, Patient A would be assigned because their oncologist consultation finished earlier. In other words, Policy 2 prioritizes the patient with the longer elapsed waiting time after consultation completion.

To implement Policy 2, new decision variables are introduced to track each patient's discharge time from the oncologist consultation. The following constraints ensure a strict sequencing between any two patients:

$$e_{ij} + e_{ji} = 1 \quad \forall i, j \in I, j > i \tag{3.24}$$

Constraints (3.24) ensure that for every pair of patients i and j, one should precede the other in the oncologist consultation discharge sequence, based on their discharge times. This ordering is enforced even when the discharge times are identical.

$$a_j + o_j \geq a_i + o_i - M(1 - e_{ij}) \quad \forall i, j \in I, j \neq i \tag{3.25}$$

Constraints (3.25) ensure that if patient i is set to precede patient j in the oncologist consultation discharge sequence, then the discharge time of patient i is not greater than that of patient j.

In the second-stage scenario subproblem formulation for SMIP-5, the constraints that need to be revised compared to SMIP-1 are (3.9)–(3.12).

Because some patients may not receive oncologist approval for chemotherapy on the day of treatment, a binary random parameter β_i^{ω} is introduced to indicate whether patient $i \in I$ is approved under scenario $\omega \in \Omega$. This parameter captures the scenario-dependent outcome of the oncologist consultation. In contrast, the drug preparation duration, k_i, is modeled as a deterministic parameter. Although patients wait during this period, it is not included in the patient waiting time (w_i^{ω}), since drug preparation is exogenous and unaffected by scheduling decisions.

The actual chemotherapy treatment start time of a patient is computed as:

$$f_i^{\omega} = a_i + o_i + \beta_i^{\omega}(k_i + w_i^{\omega}) \quad \forall i \in I \tag{3.26}$$

Similarly, the actual OCU discharge time is computed as:

$$d_i^{\omega} = f_i^{\omega} + \beta_i^{\omega}(s_i + t_i^{\omega}) \quad \forall i \in I \tag{3.27}$$

Next, the following constraints determine the feasible start times for chemotherapy treatment under each scenario:

$$f_j^{\omega} \geq f_i^{\omega} + s_i - M(5 - e_{ij} - x_{in}^{\omega} - x_{jn}^{\omega} - \beta_i^{\omega} - \beta_j^{\omega}) \quad \forall i, j \in I, j \neq i, \forall n \in N \tag{3.28}$$

Constraints (3.28) ensure that if patients i and j are both assigned to nurse n and both are approved for treatment, patient j cannot start before patient i finishes their premedication, provided i precedes j in the oncologist discharge sequence.

$$f_j^{\omega} \geq d_i^{\omega} - M(5 - e_{ij} - y_{ic}^{\omega} - y_{jc}^{\omega} - \beta_i^{\omega} - \beta_j^{\omega}) \quad \forall i, j \in I, j \neq i, \forall c \in C \tag{3.29}$$

Constraints (3.29) ensure that if patients i and j are both assigned to chair c and are approved for treatment, patient j cannot start treatment before patient i finishes.

$$f_j^{\omega} \geq f_i^{\omega} - M(3 - e_{ij} - \beta_i^{\omega} - \beta_j^{\omega}) \quad \forall i, j \in I, j \neq i \tag{3.30}$$

Constraints (3.30) indirectly reinforce the sequencing policy based on oncologist consultation discharge times. If both patients are approved and i precedes j in the oncologist discharge sequence, then patient j's chemotherapy treatment cannot start before that of patient i.

References

1. Castaing, J., et al. (2016). A stochastic programming approach to reduce patient wait times and overtime in an outpatient infusion center. *IIE Transactions on Healthcare Systems Engineering, 6*(3), 111–125.
2. Çelik, B., Gul, S., & Karsu, Ö. (2025). Maintaining fairness in stochastic chemotherapy scheduling. *Omega, 137*, 103338.
3. Demir, N. B., Gul, S., & Çelik, M. (2021). A stochastic programming approach for chemotherapy appointment scheduling. *Naval Research Logistics, 68*(1), 112–133.
4. Gul, S. (2021). Chemotherapy appointment scheduling under uncertainty by considering workload balance among nurses. *Pamukkale Üniversitesi Mühendislik Bilimleri Dergisi, 27*(4), 570–578. ISSN: 1300-7009.
5. Gul, S. (2024). Nursing care flexibility in chemotherapy appointment scheduling. *Flexible Services and Manufacturing Journal, 36*, 918–945.
6. Ireland, A., et al. (2004). The oncology nursing society ambulatory office nurse survey. *Oncology Nursing Forum, 31*(6), E147–E156.
7. Karakaya, S., Gul, S., & Çelik, M. (2023). Stochastic scheduling of chemotherapy appointments considering patient acuity levels. *European Journal of Operational Research, 305*(2), 902–916.
8. Liang, B., & Turkcan, A. (2016). Acuity-based nurse assignment and patient scheduling in oncology clinics. *Health Care Management Science, 19*, 207–226.
9. Ozyuksel, E. D., et al. (2025). Coordinating oncologist appointments with chemotherapy treatments under uncertainty. *Computers & Industrial Engineering, 204*, 111123.

Fairness in Chemotherapy Scheduling

4

Abstract

Driven by the need to incorporate fairness into both healthcare system design and service delivery, this chapter investigates various approaches to embedding fairness considerations within optimization models, with a particular emphasis on chemotherapy scheduling. It examines the key challenges involved in quantifying fairness and presents alternative functional forms that can be used either as objective functions or as constraints. The distinctions among these forms are analyzed, along with their practical implications. Furthermore, the chapter illustrates how fairness functions can be integrated into models under uncertainty, providing examples and variants of two-stage stochastic mixed-integer programming (SMIP) models to address such concerns.

4.1 Fairness in Healthcare: Key Concepts

Fairness, also referred to as equity, is a concept studied across a range of fields, including economics, (behavioral) decision-analysis, ethics, and philosophy. It is a major concern, as evidenced by the United Nations' Sustainable Development Goal of reducing inequalities, which requires actions across multiple domains [17].

Concerns about fairness naturally arise in many real-world settings, making them highly relevant to the disciplines of Operations Research (OR) and Management Science (MS). These fields apply optimization techniques to design and enhance systems efficiently and are increasingly called upon to address fairness-related challenges across diverse application domains. Examples include public service provision, humanitarian operations, telecommunication network design, healthcare services, and the allocation of critical resources such as medicines, energy, and water [4, 5, 8, 12, 14].

S. Gul, Ö. Karsu, *Chemotherapy Appointment Scheduling*, Synthesis Lectures on Operations Research and Applications, https://doi.org/10.1007/978-3-032-11552-2_4

Among these, healthcare delivery systems present a particularly urgent context in which fairness considerations are essential. A growing body of empirical research has documented significant disparities in access, affordability, and quality of care across countries and populations. As such, there is a pressing need to design healthcare systems that are equitable across multiple dimensions, including both access to services and the quality of care received.

One critical aspect of ensuring fairness in healthcare delivery lies in the monitoring and management of patient waiting times. Studies conducted in England, Spain, and Italy have revealed notable inequalities in this regard, with evidence showing that waiting times can vary significantly across different population subgroups—raising concerns about distributive justice in healthcare systems [7, 10, 13]. The results of the analysis conducted by Martin et al. [11] on ten member countries of the Organization for Economic Co-operation and Development (OECD), namely Australia, Canada, France, Germany, Netherlands, New Zealand, Norway, Sweden, Switzerland, and the United Kingdom, also indicate the existence of inequalities in waiting times for primary care in several of these countries.

Designing fair systems through optimization necessitates the quantification of equity. Although this is often challenging—since fairness is inherently context-dependent and varies across problem domains—a structured framework can still offer a meaningful way to operationalize and measure it [4, 8]. The interested reader is referred to the work by Elçi et al. [5], for an excellent guide on ways of achieving this in general optimization settings.

A central step in this process involves addressing three fundamental questions: (1) What is the good (benefit) or bad (burden) over which a fair allocation is sought? (2) To whom is the allocation made? and (3) How should the allocation be conducted? In the following section, we explore potential answers to these questions within the context of chemotherapy scheduling.

4.1.1 Input Fairness vs. Outcome Fairness

In the healthcare domain, the allocation over which fairness is sought could be service or workload related. For example, a fair chemotherapy scheduling system could ensure similar service levels and treatment quality for all patients. Alternatively, it could fairly distribute the workload among healthcare providers, such as oncologists and nurses.

More broadly, fairness considerations typically concern the allocation of either a *resource* or an *outcome*. For instance, in a vaccine allocation problem where demand exceeds supply, allocating an equal proportion of vaccines to different age groups ensures fairness in resource allocation. However, this may not lead to fair outcomes. Since the elderly population groups are at higher risk, they may require more resources to achieve similar health outcomes as younger populations. This principle applies to patients with different diseases as well; those with resource-intensive treatments will naturally require more resources to achieve equitable outcomes. Whether fairness should be pursued in the allocation of resources or in the realization of outcomes is a key design decision when integrating fairness into healthcare systems.

In chemotherapy scheduling, a central concern is achieving fairness—both in terms of equitable patient waiting times and in the balanced distribution of workloads among nurses who administer treatment. In these contexts, fairness is not applied directly to the inputs of the system, but rather evaluated based on the outcomes that result from operational decisions. This contrasts with settings where fairness is sought directly over the inputs. For example, distributing equal amounts of funding across different healthcare projects is a relatively straightforward input-based allocation. However, aiming for fairness in terms of outcomes—such as ensuring that different population groups receive equal health benefits from monetary allocations—requires a more complex approach. In such cases, one must model how resource allocation decisions translate into outcomes, often using functions or other mathematical formulations. Outcome fairness cannot be directly imposed, but must emerge as a consequence of the operational policies in place.

Chemotherapy scheduling exemplifies this challenge: waiting times for patients and workloads for nurses are not independently assigned, but are the result of the scheduling and assignment decisions made. Identifying which operational choices lead to fair outcomes is not trivial, highlighting the value of optimization methods in designing systems that promote equity in a principled and transparent manner.

4.1.2 To Whom to Be Fair?

The units to whom the decision maker aims to be fair are referred to as *entities*. These could be patients or healthcare personnel. The healthcare scheduling literature contains studies that consider fairness from each of these perspectives in contexts such as general outpatient clinic scheduling, personnel scheduling, operating room scheduling, and chemotherapy scheduling [1, 3, 6].

From a fairness perspective, it is essential to determine whether entities should be treated symmetrically or not. If the entities are indistinguishable, the anonymity principle holds. In this case, an ideally fair allocation would allocate the same amount to all entities, making any permutation of an allocation equally fair.

However, when entities differ in terms of their needs, acuity levels, entitlements, or other relevant characteristics, a fair allocation may not correspond to equal treatment. For example, if patients have varying levels of urgency or clinical priority, scheduling should reflect these differences. Consider two patients with different health statuses—one in nearly perfect health with a minor condition, and another suffering from a life-threatening complication. In such a case, the following two waiting time allocations (in minutes), which are permutations of each other, may not be perceived as equally fair: (5, 15) and (15, 5). Here, the anonymity principle is not satisfied, and any fairness function used in optimization must account for this asymmetry.

4.1.3 How to Achieve Fair Allocations?

Achieving fairness in an optimization setting requires specification of the function(s) that measure the degree of fairness in the allocations. The answers to the first two questions—what is to be fairly allocated and whom we want to treat fairly—will be instrumental in defining the function. In the next section, we explore this question for the chemotherapy scheduling problems.

4.2 Quantifying Fairness in Healthcare Delivery

Designing fair healthcare systems is a challenging task, shaped by multiple dimensions that must be carefully considered. Among the most critical are the presence of diverse stakeholders, the inherent uncertainty of healthcare environments, and the fundamental trade-off between fairness and efficiency. Each of these dimensions brings unique challenges to healthcare decision-making settings.

- *Multiple Stakeholders:* Healthcare systems involve a wide range of stakeholders, each with their own interests, needs, and perceptions of fairness. These include beneficiaries—such as patients and their families—who expect timely and equitable access to care; service providers—such as physicians, nurses, and administrative staff—who manage clinical workloads and aim to deliver quality care; and funding bodies—such as governments, insurers, or taxpayers—who are concerned with sustainability and cost-effectiveness. Because each group may define fairness differently, achieving a universally fair system requires identifying compromises that balance stakeholder priorities.

  A typical example of this trade-off is between nurse overtime and patient waiting time. A schedule that prioritizes minimizing overtime would assign appointments in a way that keeps nurses continuously occupied, potentially causing patients to wait longer for their treatment. Conversely, a schedule that focuses on minimizing patient waiting time would space out appointments so that patients are seen immediately upon arrival—this, however, could lead to idle periods for nurses and increased overtime at the end of the day.
- *Uncertainty:* Healthcare settings are often characterized by significant uncertainty, making it difficult to estimate the effects of decisions. This unpredictability becomes especially challenging in scheduling decisions, such as those in chemotherapy planning, where patients' health can be fragile and change quickly. In such settings, decisions must often be made without knowing their exact future impact. A policy that appears fair under one scenario may lead to unintended inequities under another. For this reason, fairness must be considered within a stochastic framework—one that accounts for different possible scenarios and aims for decisions that perform well across that range of possible outcomes.

- *Efficiency-Fairness Tradeoff:* Healthcare decision-making often involves balancing fairness and efficiency—two goals that do not always align. Fairness is about giving patients equitable treatment or access and ensuring a balanced distribution of workload across service providers, while efficiency focuses on making the best use of limited resources, such as time, staff, or equipment. Improving one can sometimes come at the cost of the other. Healthcare managers must carefully weigh these competing priorities and look for solutions that achieve a reasonable balance based on the system's goals and values.

The next section presents some of the widely-used functions that can be used to quantify fairness.

4.2.1 Well-known Fairness Functions Used in Service Systems

Motivated by the need to integrate fairness in various systems, a substantial body of literature has emerged on incorporating equity concerns into optimization problems [4, 8]. Broadly, this can be done through using two types of functions: *spread-based functions* that quantify the inequality in an allocation or *welfare functions* that encompass both efficiency and fairness.

Table 4.1 summarizes several widely-used fairness functions in optimization settings, using patient waiting times as an illustrative example. We assume that there are n patients and w_i shows the waiting time of patient $i \in I$. Common functions include the minmax function (Rawlsian approach), the range, sum of pairwise differences (SoPD), variance, mean absolute deviation (MAD), Hoover index, the Gini coefficient and the Ordered weighted averaging (OWA) functions.

The functions except the minmax (Rawlsian), OWA functions, and the equity and efficiency encouraging metric (EEEM) [3] can be considered spread-based. Among these, the Gini coefficient is an inequality measure. OWA functions constitute a set of social welfare functions characterized by a set of rank-dependent weights, of which Rawlsian function is a special case. We, however, provide the Rawlsian approach separately; as it is widely adopted in many optimization settings to incorporate fairness concerns. EEEM is a function that considers both efficiency and spread, as recently discussed by Celik et al. [3]. In case of allocations of undesirable outcomes such as waiting time, all these functions except the EEEM, are to be minimized.

4.2.1.1 Spread-based Functions

Spread-based functions often rely on statistical or inequality measures to assess how evenly outcomes—such as waiting times—are distributed among individuals. These functions can be incorporated either as additional objectives or as constraints within an optimization model.

Table 4.1 Fairness functions in a deterministic setting. These functions can be used as objectives or in constraints. The ones that do not capture efficiency can be combined with functions emphasizing efficiency in a multiobjective framework

Function	Expression	Notes
Rawlsian	$\max_{i\in I} w_i$	Easy to formulate, widely used, fails to distinguish allocations with the same maximum element.
Range	$\max_{i\in I} w_i$ - $\min_{i\in I} w_i$	Easy-to-formulate, focuses only on the difference between the worst and best entity. Can be normalized by dividing by the mean.
Sum of pairwise differences	$\sum_{i,j\in I:j>i} \|w_i - w_j\|$	Easy-to-formulate, has been used in outpatient scheduling, can be considered as an attempt to measure total *envy*.
Variance	$\frac{1}{n}\sum_{i\in I}(w_i - \bar{w})^2$	Not commonly used, one reason is its nonlinear form. Equivalently, standard deviation can be used, which turns into coefficient of variation when normalized using the mean.
Mean absolute deviation	$\frac{1}{n}\sum_{i\in I} \|w_i - \bar{w}\|$	Can be normalized by dividing by the mean, which is called relative mean deviation.
Gini	$\frac{\sum_{i,j\in I:j>i} \|w_i - w_j\|}{n\sum_{i\in I} w_i}$	Inequality metric: Satisfies Pigou-Dalton, scale independence and population independence axioms. Scales between 0 and 1. Proportional to the area between the Lorenz curve and the line of perfect equality.
Hoover index	$\frac{\sum_{i\in I} \|w_i - \bar{w}\|}{\sum_{i\in I} w_i}$	Proportional to the maximum vertical distance between the Lorenz curve and the line of perfect equality. Note that using this index is equivalent to using relative mean deviation, i.e. mean absolute deviation divided by the mean.
Ordered weighted averaging	$\sum_{i\in I} \alpha_i \overleftarrow{w}_i$	α is a rank-based weight vector satisfying: $\alpha_1 \geq \alpha_2 \geq \ldots \geq \alpha_n$. $\overleftarrow{w}$ denotes the non-increasingly ordered permutation of vector of w. OWA functions form a set of parametric social welfare functions. The nonlinear expression is linearizable using additional decision variables and constraints. The rank-based weights may be difficult to set.
Equity and efficiency encouraging metric	$\alpha \in (0, 1]$ s.t. $\eta + \frac{1}{\|I\|(1-\alpha)}\sum_{i\in I}[w_i - \eta]_+ \leq \tau$	The highest level α, such that the weighted average of the worst $(1-\alpha)$-quantile waiting times across all patients does not exceed a predefined threshold τ.

Inequality metrics have been extensively studied in the economics literature [15]. These metrics are used to quantify inequality as they satisfy a set of well-established and widely accepted axiomatic properties. One key property is the *Pigou-Dalton principle of transfers*, which states that if a small amount of a resource is transferred from a better-off entity to a worse-off one—without reversing their relative positions—then the inequality measure should reflect an improvement.

By definition, inequality metrics are symmetric, meaning they assign the same value to all permutations of a given allocation. Other important properties include scale independence (the metric should not change if all values are proportionally scaled) and population independence (the metric should be invariant to replication of the population). For instance, a metric satisfying scale independence would give the same value to (15, 10) and (30, 20); and one satisfying population independence would assign the same value to (15, 10) and (15, 10, 15, 10, 15, 10) as the population of the first allocation is simply replicated in the latter. Gini coefficient satisfies both of these axioms, hence the Gini coefficients of all these allocations are the same.

Inequality metrics and normalized forms of the spread based functions, such as relative mean deviation and coefficient of variation, quantify only the distribution without considering the efficiency of the system. As a result, they cannot serve as the sole objective in optimization. For instance, a scenario where all patients experience extremely long but equal waiting times would be considered perfectly fair by these metrics, even though such an outcome is clearly unacceptable from a service quality perspective.

This limitation can be seen in Table 4.2, which presents how nine example schedules perform with respect to alternative fairness functions. Schedule 9 is considered perfectly fair under spread-based metrics but would not be implemented in practice due to its inefficiency.

Table 4.2 Quantifying fairness through spread-based functions: choice of the metric might affect the ranking of the alternatives. A perfectly fair allocation may be highly inefficient. *TWT* Total waiting time (minutes)

	Patient waiting times					Efficiency	Fairness function					
Schedule	1	2	3	4	5	TWT	Range	SoPD	Variance	MAD	Hoover index	Gini
1	5	0	20	10	15	50	20	100	62.50	6.00	0.60	0.40
2	10	5	10	15	15	55	10	50	17.50	3.20	0.29	0.18
3	13	8	13	11	10	55	5	26	4.50	1.60	0.15	0.09
4	11	10	14	10	10	55	4	18	3.00	1.20	0.11	0.07
5	10	5	12.5	15	17.5	60	12.5	60	23.13	3.60	0.30	0.20
6	12.5	10	10	10	17.5	60	7.5	35	10.63	2.40	0.20	0.12
7	12.5	16.5	12.5	16	12.5	70	4	23	4.25	1.80	0.13	0.07
8	15	15	15	15	10	70	5	20	5.00	1.60	0.11	0.06
9	20	20	20	20	20	100	0	0	0.00	0.00	0.00	0.00

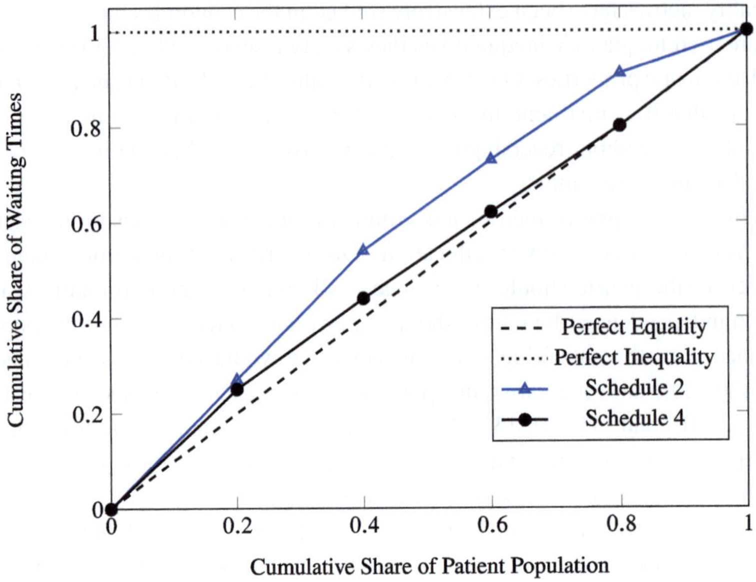

Fig. 4.1 Lorenz curves of Schedules 2 and 4. Both have the same total waiting time, but Schedule 4 exhibits a more equitable allocation across patients, placing it closer to the line of perfect equality (*dashed diagonal*)

Spread based functions can, however, be used as additional objectives or in the constraints. They are especially useful when comparing allocations that have the same efficiency level, such as the same total waiting times. For example, in Table 4.2, Schedules 2 and 4 yield identical total waiting times, but Schedule 4 is more equitable, with lower values across all fairness metrics.

Schedule 4's better performance can also be seen in Fig. 4.1, which shows the Lorenz curves of the two schedules. The Lorenz curve graphically shows how an outcome is allocated across the population, compared to a perfectly equal allocation. It visualizes the cumulative share of the outcome received by different proportions of the population, when recipients are ordered from the worst-off to the best-off. Table 4.3 shows the corresponding calculations. The difference is also reflected in their Gini coefficient values. Gini coefficient is the ratio of the area between the line of perfect equality and the observed Lorenz curve to the area between the line of perfect equality and the line of perfect inequality (see the horizontal, dashed line in Fig. 4.1).

It is also important to note that while different spread-based metrics may be correlated, they do not always rank allocations in the same order. This indicates that the selection of the fairness metric can significantly influence both the evaluation and the outcome of the optimization process.

Table 4.3 Lorenz Curve calculations. In each schedule, patients are ordered from the worst-off to the best-off. *CSoPP* Cumulative share of patient population, *WT* Waiting time (minutes), *CWT* Cumulative waiting time (minutes), *CSoWT* Cumulative share of waiting time

Schedule 2					Schedule 4				
Patient	CSoPP	WT	CWT	CSoWT	Patient	CSoPP	WT	CWT	CSoWT
4	0.2	15	15	0.27	3	0.2	14	14	0.25
5	0.4	15	30	0.55	1	0.4	11	25	0.45
1	0.6	10	40	0.73	2	0.6	10	35	0.64
3	0.8	10	50	0.91	4	0.8	10	45	0.82
2	1.0	5	55	1.00	5	1.0	10	55	1.00

Multiobjective Frameworks Overall, the inherent trade-off between efficiency and fairness becomes clear: achieving a fair schedule may come at the cost of reduced efficiency. Balancing these two concerns is important to ensure both the quality of care and patient satisfaction.

One effective way to integrate both considerations into chemotherapy scheduling is through *multiobjective optimization*. For example, minimizing both the total waiting time (an efficiency measure) and the Gini coefficient (a fairness metric) allows for capturing this balance explicitly. Using biobjective programming, a Pareto set of solutions can be obtained, which would reveal the trade-off between these two criteria. Decision-makers can then select from among the Pareto-optimal schedules based on their preferences. Alternatively, if preferences are known in advance, a single solution can be obtained by defining a trade-off using weighted objectives—for instance, optimizing a weighted sum of total waiting time and the Gini coefficient. Another approach is to optimize efficiency (total waiting time) while enforcing a constraint on fairness—e.g., minimizing total waiting time subject to a bound on the Gini coefficient or other inequality measure.

4.2.1.2 Social Welfare Functions

Functions that capture both efficiency and fairness are often formulated as *social welfare functions*. When anonymity is assumed (i.e., the identity of the entities is irrelevant), these functions are symmetric and satisfy Pigou-Dalton principle of transfers, at least in the weak sense. That is, the functions should be in line with the concept of equitable dominance, also referred to as Generalized Lorenz (GL) dominance [16], which is defined below for waiting time allocation vectors.

Definition 4.1 For two waiting time allocation vectors $w^1 \in \mathbb{R}^n$ and $w^2 \in \mathbb{R}^n$, w^1 equitably dominates w^2 iff $\sum_{i=1}^{k} \overleftarrow{w}_i^1 \leq \sum_{i=1}^{k} \overleftarrow{w}_i^2 \;\; \forall k \in \{1, \ldots, n\}$ and $\sum_{i=1}^{k} \overleftarrow{w}_i^1 < \sum_{i=1}^{k} \overleftarrow{w}_i^2$ for some $k \in \{1, \ldots, n\}$. Here, $\overleftarrow{w}$ denotes the non-increasingly ordered permutation of vector w [9].

To evaluate equitable dominance, one compares the cumulative ordered vectors of two allocations. Due to the symmetry property, using ordered permutations preserves preference ordering. For example, consider again Schedules 2 and 4. The ordered waiting time vector of Schedule 2 is (15, 15, 10, 10, 5), while that of Schedule 4 is (14, 11, 10, 10, 10). The cumulative sums of these vectors are:
Schedule 2: (15, 30, 40, 50, 55)
Schedule 4: (14, 25, 35, 45, 55)

As we compare each cumulative sum from $k = \{1, \ldots, 5\}$, we find that Schedule 2 has higher values at every point, except the final total, which is equal. Thus, Schedule 4 equitably dominates Schedule 2. A well-behaved social welfare function—one that satisfies GL dominance—would not assign a higher score to Schedule 2 than to Schedule 4, as formally stated in Remark 4.1.

Remark 4.1 When a disbenefit (such as waiting time) is allocated, a function $W(w)$ is an equitable aggregation function if the following condition holds:
For any $w^1 \in \mathbb{R}^n$ and $w^2 \in \mathbb{R}^n$, $W(w^1) \leq W(w^2) \iff w^1$ equitably dominates w^2.

In the healthcare domain, Ordered Weighted Averaging (OWA) functions have been proposed as suitable equitable aggregation functions that incorporate both efficiency and fairness considerations [2]. These functions evaluate the total penalty of a waiting time allocation by assigning weights based on the rank order of individual waiting times. That is, higher weights (or penalties) are assigned to longer waiting times, reflecting a stronger concern for the worst-off patients. The waiting time of the patient waiting the most (resp. the least) has the highest (resp. lowest) penalty coefficient.

OWA functions offer a flexible modeling approach, where different weighting schemes reflect different managerial priorities. Two extremes in the OWA family are the *Rawlsian* and *Utilitarian* functions. The Rawlsian function focuses exclusively on the worst-off individual by assigning an infinitely large weight to the maximum waiting time—effectively minimizing the maximum wait. In contrast, the Utilitarian approach assigns equal weights to all individuals, reducing the OWA function to the total waiting time and emphasizing system-wide efficiency over fairness.

Table 4.4 presents several example OWA functions, each defined by a distinct set of rank-based weights which, without loss of generality, are normalized to sum to one. Table 4.5 reports the corresponding welfare levels for the nine example schedules, evaluated using these OWA functions. Among these, only schedules 1, 3, and 4 represent equitably nondominated allocations, i.e. they are not equitably dominated by any other allocation in the set.

Specifically, Schedule 1 performs best under a utilitarian social welfare function, as it achieves the lowest total waiting time. In contrast, Schedule 3 is optimal from a Rawlsian perspective, minimizing the maximum individual waiting time. Schedule 4 offers a balanced compromise between these extremes.

Table 4.4 Example functions from the OWA family for the example with five entities (patients)

Function	Weights
OWA1: Utilitarian	(0.2,0.2,0.2,0.2,0.2)
OWA2	(0.23,0.22,0.2,0.2,0.15)
OWA3	(0.4,0.25,0.2,0.1,0.05)
OWA4	(0.6,0.15,0.1,0.05)
OWA5: Rawlsian	(1,0,0,0,0)

Table 4.5 Using OWA functions to quantify social welfare. These functions encompass both efficiency and fairness. For each OWA function, the best value is shown in **bold**

	Ordered waiting times					OWA values				
Schedule	1	2	3	4	5	OWA1	OWA2	OWA3	OWA4	OWA5
1	20	15	10	5	0	**10**	**10.90**	14.25	15.75	20
2	15	15	10	10	5	11	11.50	13.00	13.50	15
3	13	13	11	10	8	11	11.25	12.05	**12.25**	**13**
4	14	11	10	10	10	11	11.14	**11.85**	12.55	14
5	17.5	15	12.5	10	5	12	12.58	14.50	15.25	17.5
6	17.5	12.5	10	10	10	12	12.28	13.63	14.88	17.5
7	16.5	16	12.5	12.5	12.5	14	14.19	14.98	15.43	16.5
8	15	15	15	15	10	14	14.25	14.75	14.75	15
9	20	20	20	20	20	20	20.00	20.00	20.00	20

Recall that Schedule 4 equitably dominates Schedule 2: it has better (lower) OWA values than Schedule 2, regardless of the weights used, except the Utilitarian case. This observation aligns with Remark 4.1.

Recently, a new performance function has been introduced for CAS, which jointly considers both efficiency and fairness in the evaluation of patient waiting time allocations [3]. In Table 4.1, we present the formulation of this function for the deterministic case, and provide a detailed discussion for its use in stochastic environments in Sect. 4.3.

4.2.2 Fairness in Stochastic Settings

When the waiting time allocations are deterministic, i.e. when there is no uncertainty in the system, the fairness functions discussed above can be directly applied to quantify and incorporate fairness into scheduling decisions. In contrast, in a stochastic setting, fairness analysis becomes more complex. A schedule is no longer associated with a single, known waiting time vector, but rather with a distribution of possible waiting time allocations across multiple scenarios. This uncertainty introduces new challenges in evaluating and comparing schedules from a fairness perspective.

Table 4.6 Waiting times for two schedules in a setting with 5 patients and 4 scenarios

(a) Schedule 1

	Patients				
Scenarios	1	2	3	4	5
1	15	5	17.5	20	0
2	10	5	10	5	0
3	5	5	5	0	0
4	10	5	12.5	5	0

(b) Schedule 2

	Patients				
Scenarios	1	2	3	4	5
1	10	5	12.5	20	0
2	15	5	5	5	0
3	10	5	10	5	0
4	5	5	17.5	0	0

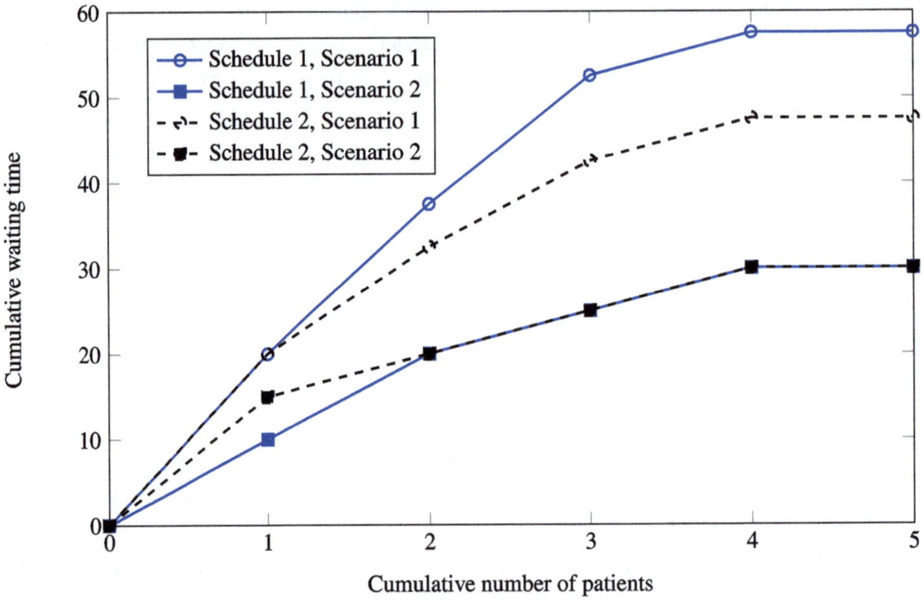

Fig. 4.2 Generalized Lorenz curves for example Schedules 1 and 2 in Scenarios 1 and 2

To illustrate this, consider a simple example in which two schedules are evaluated under uncertainty. Suppose that for each schedule, there are four equally likely scenarios, as shown in Table 4.6. From any patient's perspective, these two schedules are equivalent, as the waiting times are permutations of each other.

However, these schedules yield different waiting time allocations in each realization. While one schedule may perform better in a particular scenario, the other may be better in another, as seen in Fig. 4.2. The figure depicts the GL Curves, which plot the cumulative sums of the allocations ordered from largest to smallest without normalization. Unlike standard Lorenz curves, these curves capture both the inequality and the overall scale of the allocations. Given two waiting time allocations with different GL curves, one equitably dominates another if its GL curve does not lie above that of the other allocation at any point. As observed, in Scenario 1, Schedule 2 equitably dominates Schedule 1, whereas in Scenario 2, Schedule 1 equitably dominates Schedule 2.

If these two schedules are compared using ex-ante measures such as expected total waiting time or allocation of expected waiting times, they would be indistinguishable. Yet, their performances under different realizations are notably different. Therefore, we propose managing fairness by evaluating the waiting time allocations ex-post, i.e., assessing the fairness of each realized allocation across all scenarios individually. This approach avoids relying solely on aggregate expected values. Compared to an ex-ante approach—which evaluates fairness based only on expected figures—the ex-post evaluation provides a more comprehensive and robust measure of fairness under uncertainty.

4.3 Incorporating Fairness Criteria into Chemotherapy Scheduling Models

In this section we will discuss variants of SMIP-1, obtained by explicitly incorporating fairness using some of the metrics presented in previous sections. We will discuss the use of two widely-used metrics:

- The Gini coefficient, as a representative inequality metric, and
- The Rawlsian criterion, which is popular for its intuitive interpretation and emphasis on the worst-off.

We will then discuss the use of EEEM that has been recently shown to be effective in establishing fair and efficient schedules.

4.3.1 Gini Coefficient

To limit the Gini coefficient in every scenario so that it does not exceed a predefined threshold G, the following constraint is added to the optimization model:

$$\frac{\sum_{i,j \in I: j>i} |w_j^{\omega} - w_i^{\omega}|}{|I| \sum_{i \in I} w_i^{\omega}} \leq G \quad \forall \omega \in \Omega \tag{4.1}$$

While this expression is nonlinear due to the absolute values and division, it can be linearized using auxiliary variables representing the absolute differences. Enforcing this constraint for every scenario adopts a risk-averse perspective, ensuring fairness under all possible outcomes. We refer to SMIP-1 with this set of constraints as SMIP-6. Alternatively, a chance-constrained relaxation could be considered to allow controlled violations with a certain probability.

4.3.2 Rawlsian

The Rawlsian fairness approach focuses on minimizing the maximum waiting time faced by any patient across all scenarios. This can be implemented by imposing an upper bound R on the waiting times as follows:

$$w_i^\omega \leq R \quad \forall i \in I, \forall \omega \in \Omega \tag{4.2}$$

We refer to SMIP-1 with this set of constraints as SMIP-7. This constraint can be easily adopted to settings where thresholds differ for different patient categories.

4.3.3 Equity and Efficiency Encouraging Metric (EEEM)

The EEEM is based on Conditional Value-at-Risk (CVaR) and specifically focuses on preventing excessive patient waiting times in each scenario [3]. It is defined as the highest confidence level α such that the weighted average of the worst $(1 - \alpha)$-quantile waiting times across all patients does not exceed a predefined threshold τ in every scenario. That is, EEEM $= \inf_{\omega \in \Omega}(\alpha^\omega)$, which satisfy the following set of inequalities for given bound τ and which are in the interval [0,1).

$$\eta^\omega + \frac{1}{|I|(1-\alpha^\omega)} \sum_{i \in I} [w_i^\omega - \eta^\omega]_+ \leq \tau \quad \forall \omega \in \Omega \tag{4.3}$$

In this approach, EEEM provides information on the percentile up to which patients are protected against unacceptable waiting times.

This protection can be incorporated in different ways. One can predetermine a confidence level α and minimize the weighted average of $(1 - \alpha) \times |I|$ of the highest waiting times across all scenarios given α. This would be in line with the CVaR metric. For a given confidence level α, CVaR of random variable W is defined as follows:

$$\text{CVaR}_\alpha(W) = \min_\eta \left\{ \eta + \frac{1}{1-\alpha} \mathbb{E}\left[(W - \eta)^+\right] \right\}.$$

This is a minimization problem, where optimality is attained at a specific value of η, called the Value at Risk (VaR), and given by:

$$\text{VaR}_\alpha(W) = \min \{\eta : F_W(\eta) > \alpha\}.$$

The α value, however, may not be easy to determine. An alternative approach would be maximizing the confidence level α to ensure that the weighted average of waiting times

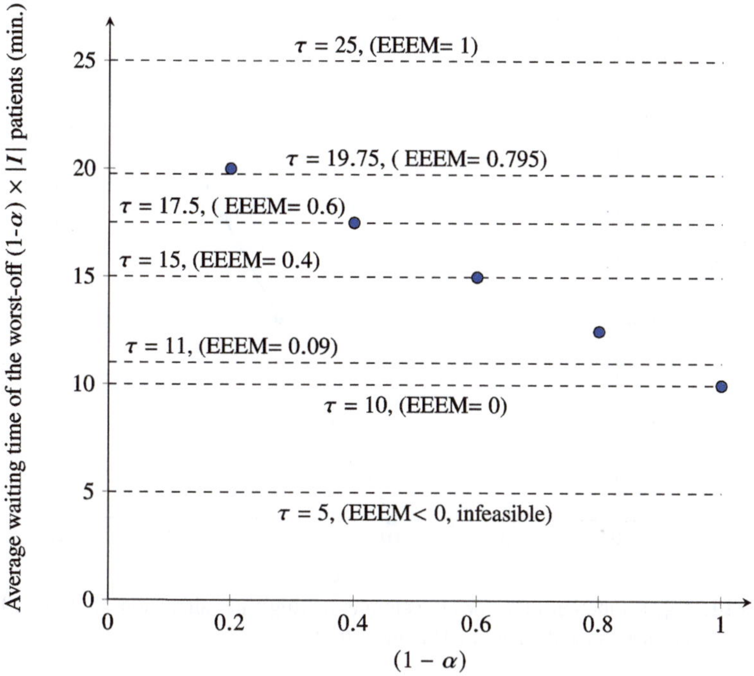

Fig. 4.3 EEEM calculation for an example waiting time allocation of (5, 0, 20, 10, 15)

for $(1 - \alpha) \times |I|$ of the longest waiting patients does not exceed a predetermined upper limit in each scenario. This is what EEEM strives to achieve.

We exemplify the metric on an example allocation, corresponding to Schedule 1 of Table 4.2. For ease of demonstration, we consider the deterministic case; that is we assume that there is only one scenario and hence we remove the scenario index ω from the discussion. This schedule results in an ordered waiting time vector of (20, 15, 10, 5, 0). Figure 4.3 shows the average waiting time incurred by the worst-off $(1 - \alpha) \times |I|$ patients for different values of α.

The parameter τ determines the highest level of α, the EEEM value, corresponding to the allocation. For example, when τ is set to 25 (or to any value ≥ 20 minutes), all waiting times fall below this threshold, hence α is (almost) 1. As τ becomes stricter, the EEEM value of the schedule decreases. When τ is set to 15 minutes, the average of the two $(5 \times (1 - 0.6))$ largest waiting times is still above the threshold, hence α cannot be 0.6. In this case, the largest α satisfying Eq. (4.3) is 0.4. Note that the value of η is, by definition, less than or equal to the threshold τ; and the η value that yields the maximum α in this case is 10. When τ is 11 minutes, we see that the average of the longest four $(5 \times (1 - 0.2))$ waiting times is still above this threshold and the overall average, $(50/5 \times (1 - 0))$, is below the threshold. Here, the largest α satisfying Eq. (4.3) is 0.09 $(\frac{50}{5\times(1-0.09)} = 11)$, and the corresponding η is 0. Finally, if $\tau = 10$, the EEEM value becomes 0, as the

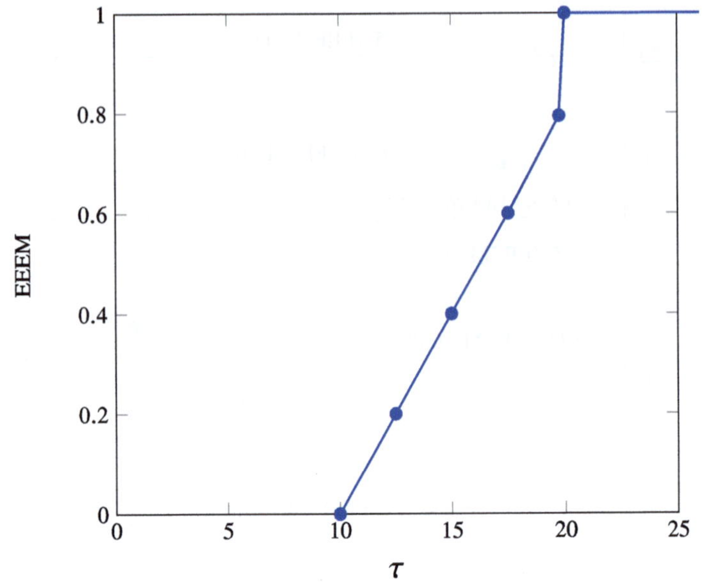

Fig. 4.4 EEEM as a function of τ for an example waiting time allocation of (5, 0, 20, 10, 15). EEEM score decreases as the threshold τ becomes stricter

threshold corresponds exactly to the average waiting time. Again, the corresponding η is 0. Figure 4.4 shows EEEM as a function of τ for the example allocation.

Note that EEEM is based on a *weighted* average time calculation; hence the maximum α does not necessarily take discrete values that are multiples of $1/|I|$, but instead take any (non-discrete) value in the interval [0,1), especially when the τ threshold lies between two average waiting time values.

Finally, Fig. 4.5 shows the average waiting times of the worst-off $(1 - \alpha) \times |I|$ patients for different values of α, for the example Schedules 2 and 4 of Table 4.2. Recall that Schedule 4 equitably dominates Schedule 2. In line with this, for any choice of threshold τ, Schedule 4 is at least as good as Schedule 2 with respect to EEEM; and it is strictly better when $11 < \tau < 15$.

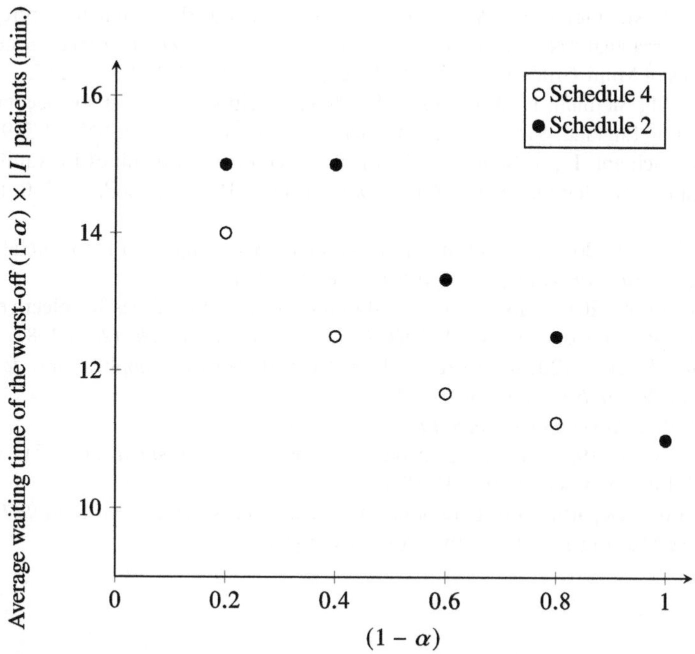

Fig. 4.5 EEEM calculation for waiting time allocations of Schedules 2 and 4 of Table 4.2. For any threshold τ, Schedule 4 is at least as good as Schedule 2 with respect to EEEM

References

1. Ahmadi-Javid, A., Jalali, Z., & Klassen, K. J. (2017). Outpatient appointment systems in healthcare: A review of optimization studies. *European Journal of Operational Research, 258*(1), 3–34.
2. Argyris, N., Karsu, Ö., & Yavuz, M. (2022). Fair resource allocation: Using welfare-based dominance constraints. *European Journal of Operational Research, 297*(2), 560–578. ISSN: 0377-2217.
3. Çelik, B., Gul, S., & Karsu, Ö. (2025). Maintaining fairness in stochastic chemotherapy scheduling. *Omega, 137*, 103338.
4. Chen, V. X., & Hooker, J. N. (2023). A guide to formulating fairness in an optimization model. *Annals of Operations Research, 326*(1), 581–619.
5. Elçi, Ö., Hooker, J., & Zhang, P. (2025). *The structure of fair solutions achieving fairness in an optimization model.* https://link.springer.com/book/10.1007/978-3-031-82190-5#bibliographic-information
6. Fuchs, G., Schimmelpfeng, K., & Brunner, J. O. (2025). A roadmap for integrating fairness in personnel planning and scheduling in hospitals. *Operations Research, Data Analytics and Logistics*, 200479.
7. García-Corchero, J. D., & Jiménez-Rubio, D. (2022). Waiting times in healthcare: Equal treatment for equal need? *International Journal for Equity in Health, 21*(1), 184.
8. Karsu, Ö., & Morton, A. (2015). Inequity averse optimization in operational research. *European Journal of Operational Research, 245*(2), 343–359.

9. Kostreva, M. M., Ogryczak, W. L., & Wierzbicki, A. (2004). Equitable aggregations and multiple criteria analysis. *European Journal of Operational Research, 158*(2). Methodological Foundations of Multi-Criteria Decision Making, pp. 362–377. ISSN: 0377-2217.
10. Laudicella, M., Siciliani, L., & Cookson, R. (2012). Waiting times and socioeconomic status: Evidence from England. *Social Science Medicine, 74*(9), 1331–1341. ISSN: 0277-9536.
11. Martin, S., Siciliani, L., & Smith, P. (2020). Socioeconomic inequalities in waiting times for primary care across ten OECD countries. *Social Science Medicine, 263*, 113230. ISSN: 0277-9536.
12. Näher, A.-F., et al. (2024). Measuring fairness preferences is important for artificial intelligence in health care. *The Lancet Digital Health, 6*(5), e302–e304.
13. Petrelli, A., et al. (2012). Socioeconomic differences in waiting times for elective surgery: A population-based retrospective study. *BMC Health Services Research, 12*(1), 268.
14. Petropoulos, F., et al. (2024). Operational research: Methods and applications. *Journal of the Operational Research Society, 75*(3), 423–617.
15. Sen, A. (1997). *On economic inequality*. Oxford University Press.
16. Shorrocks, A. F. (1983). Ranking income distributions. *Economica, 50*(197), 3–17. ISSN: 00130427, 14680335 (Visited on 04/21/2025).
17. United Nations: Department of Economic and Social Affairs. (2025). *Sustainable Development Goals*. Accessed Aug 18, 2025. https://sdgs.un.org/goals.

Case Study 5

Abstract

This chapter demonstrates the application of mathematical modeling tools to chemotherapy scheduling, using real-world data from an Outpatient Chemotherapy Unit (OCU). Example schedules generated through two-stage stochastic mixed-integer programming (SMIP) formulations are used to illustrate the problem dynamics and the impact of stochasticity on system performance. These examples highlight how an OCU manager can explore and balance typically conflicting objectives—such as operational efficiency, patient equity, and equitable workload distribution among nurses—by adjusting model parameters. Finally, the schedules produced by the mathematical models are compared to a baseline schedule currently used in practice, demonstrating improvements across multiple performance dimensions.

5.1 Scheduling Practices and Dataset from the OCU at Hacettepe Oncology Hospital

This case study examines the scheduling practices at the OCU of Hacettepe University Oncology Hospital in Ankara, Turkey [2]. The OCU contains 32 chairs, 28 of which are allocated for chemotherapy treatments and the remaining 4 for supportive care. On a typical day, the unit serves between 60 and 85 patients, with 10 nurses providing care.

Patients are treated in two shifts, separated by a lunch break: the morning shift runs from 08:00 to 12:00, and the afternoon shift from 13:00 to 17:00. The head nurse is responsible for preparing the daily schedule.

Oncologist consultations and laboratory tests are conducted the day before treatment. As a result, patients are assigned appointment times only for their chemotherapy sessions. The head nurse allocates patients to four main appointment slots: two in the morning

S. Gul, Ö. Karsu, *Chemotherapy Appointment Scheduling*, Synthesis Lectures on Operations Research and Applications, https://doi.org/10.1007/978-3-032-11552-2_5

Table 5.1 Predicted treatment duration intervals, actual infusion duration intervals, and probability of occurrence for each patient category

Category	Predicted treatment (min)	Probability (%)	Actual infusion (min)
1	$20 < t \leq 45$	26.96	[16, 44]
2	$45 < t \leq 100$	7.85	[29, 80]
3	$100 < t \leq 150$	33.33	[74, 132]
4	$150 < t \leq 240$	31.86	[125, 217]

(08:00 and 10:30) and two in the afternoon (13:00 and 15:30). Patients with longer expected treatment durations are assigned to the first slot of each shift to minimize overtime, while those with shorter treatments are placed in the second slot. In rare cases, when a treatment is expected to exceed 270 minutes, it is split into two parts—one administered in the morning and the remainder in the afternoon.

The OCU is organized into several small rooms, each containing 2–4 chairs to allow nurses to closely monitor patients. One or two nurses are assigned to each room, with 7–8 patients typically scheduled per room in a given shift. In this case study, we focus on the scheduling of a single room.

Patients are classified into four categories based on their predicted treatment durations. This categorization is used when sampling infusion durations from the dataset. Since the 95% confidence interval for premedication durations is narrow [14.61, 16.09], we fix the premedication duration at 15 minutes for all patients and scenarios, and only sample infusion durations [1, 3–5]. The sampling process begins by generating a random number to determine the patient's category according to the probability of occurrence of each category. Next, an infusion duration is randomly drawn from the actual infusion durations observed for that category. For each patient, the number of sampled infusion durations equals the number of scenarios considered. Table 5.1 presents the predicted treatment duration intervals, actual infusion duration intervals, and the corresponding probability of occurrence for each patient category in the dataset.

5.2 Example Scheduling Solutions

To demonstrate the dynamics of the chemotherapy scheduling problem and explore the properties of various scheduling solutions, we present a small illustrative example. This example considers a single-room scheduling instance involving 7 patients, 3 infusion chairs, and 2 nurses. The model incorporates uncertainty in infusion durations through a set of scenarios. For ease of illustration, we limit the instance to only five possible scenarios. The infusion duration data for each patient under each scenario is provided in Table 5.2.

We find scheduling solutions to this instance by solving SMIP-1 with a mixed integer programming solver (CPLEX 22.1.1). As the OCU prioritizes (expected) overtime reduction over expected total waiting time reduction, we set the trade-off parameter λ as

Table 5.2 Infusion durations in scenarios (minutes)

Patients	Scenarios 1	2	3	4	5
1	105	64	42	38	120
2	21	118	29	120	129
3	40	27	123	139	124
4	22	153	127	117	143
5	96	114	128	24	118
6	150	118	98	55	22
7	130	20	90	32	111

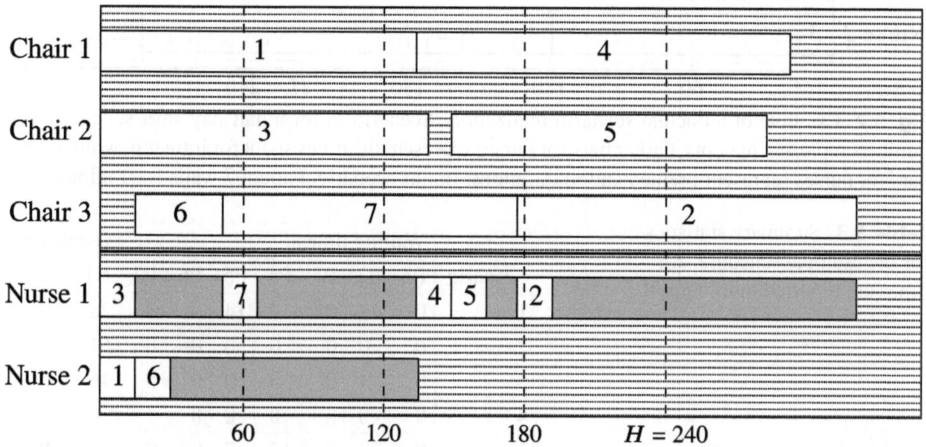

Fig. 5.1 Example of an actual scenario realization (Scenario 5) for a half-day shift schedule. The numbers represent patients, darker bars for nurses represent the times spent for infusion, while lighter bars for nurses represent premedication durations. In this scenario, Patients 2, 4, and 5 wait for 20, 15, and 7 minutes, respectively

0.3. Below, we discuss different solutions that can be obtained under different parameter settings.

Note that SMIP-1 is a stochastic programming problem, a class of problems well-known to be computationally challenging. There are excellent works proposing methods that can be used for finding high quality heuristic schedules or optimal schedules in reasonable time. For the sake of brevity, we obtained a feasible schedule by solving SMIP-1 with a 200 seconds time limit, setting the upper bound on the overtime (L) to 90 minutes. This solution sets the patient appointment times as follows: $a_1 = 0$, $a_2 = 158$, $a_3 = 0$, $a_4 = 120$, $a_5 = 143$, $a_6 = 15$, $a_7 = 52$. Note that this schedule would involve different nurse and chair assignments in each scenario. In Fig. 5.1, we provide Gantt Chart for a specific scenario, Scenario 5. In this scenario, Chair 1 serves Patients 1 and 4; Chair 2 serves Patients 3 and 5, while Chair 3 serves Patients 2, 6 and 7. Nurse 1 serves Patients 2–5, and 7, while Nurse 2 serves Patients 1 and 6. In this scenario, Patients 2, 4, and 5 wait for 20, 15, and 7 minutes, respectively.

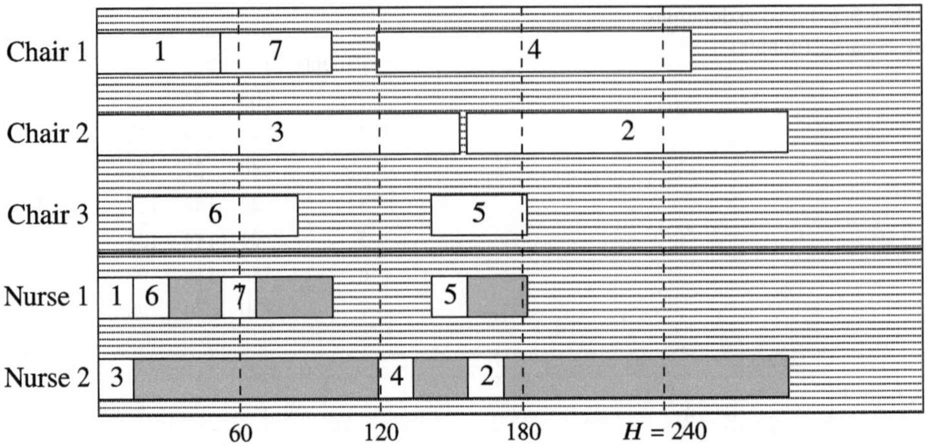

Fig. 5.2 Example of an actual scenario realization (Scenario 4) for a half-day shift schedule. The numbers represent patients, darker bars for nurses represent the times spent for infusion, while lighter bars for nurses represent premedication durations. In this scenario, Patient 7 waits for 1 minute

Table 5.3 Summary statistics for the example schedule. All times are reported in minutes

	Waiting times							Overtimes	
Scenario	P1	P2	P3	P4	P5	P6	P7	N1	N2
1	0	22	0	0	14	0	3	28	0
2	0	0	0	0	0	0	0	51	0
3	0	4	0	8	0	0	5	46	0
4	0	0	0	0	0	0	1	0	53
5	0	20	0	15	7	0	0	82	0

The assignments in another scenario (Scenario 4) differ and are depicted in Fig. 5.2. In this scenario, the only waiting time of one minute is incurred by Patient 7.

Table 5.3 shows the summary of the performance measures for this solution. While this schedule performs quite well in Scenario 4, it may lead to significantly worse waiting times if Scenario 5 is realized. Moreover, the nurse overtime figures can be unacceptably high, with one of the nurses having an overtime of more than one hour in one of these scenarios. This example demonstrates the challenge that stochasticity brings into this problem.

Moreover, it shows that ensuring equity (fairness) only in expected figures may not be meaningful; as the realized waiting time allocations may involve high degrees of inequality under some scenarios, deeming the solution undesirable in practice. The manager may seek an acceptable solution, for example, through preventing schedules resulting in highly unequal waiting time allocations across patients.

The solution summarized in Table 5.3 results in Gini coefficient values ranging between 0 and 0.86 in different scenarios. When we limit the Gini coefficient to be at most 0.5 in any scenario, and solve SMIP-6, we obtain another schedule ($a_1 = 191$, $a_2 = 0$, $a_3 = 52$, $a_4 = 126$, $a_5 = 145$, $a_6 = 15$, $a_7 = 0$), in which none of the patients wait in any of the scenarios.

Table 5.4 Summary statistics for an example schedule when overtime is limited by 60 minutes (a_1= 165, a_2= 15, a_3= 0, a_4= 113, a_5= 150, a_6= 0, a_7= 39). All times are reported in minutes

	Waiting times							Overtimes	
Scenario	P1	P2	P3	P4	P5	P6	P7	N1	N2
1	0	0	0	0	0	0	12	0	45
2	0	0	0	0	0	0	3	0	41
3	0	0	0	0	0	0	20	53	0
4	0	0	0	4	0	0	31	9	0
5	0	0	0	26	9	0	0	60	52

Yet, in this case, the overtime figures of the nurses increase significantly, with Nurse 1 having an overtime of 54 and 48 minutes in two scenarios, while Nurse 2 having possible overtimes of 71, 18 and 86 minutes. This results in an approximately 6.5% increase in the expected overtime. Similarly, when we limit the maximum waiting time to be 15 minutes and solve SMIP-7 (SMIP-1 with the Rawlsian type fairness constraints), we again obtain a schedule, where no patient waits in any scenario, but one nurse has an overtime as high as 86 minutes.

To avoid undesirably high overtimes, the maximum overtime allowed can be reduced, allowing a better workload balance over nurses. In this example problem, when overtime is limited by 60 minutes, another schedule can be obtained, which has the results shown in Table 5.4. In this solution, the expected overtime stays the same compared to the SMIP-1 solution with an overtime bound of 90 minutes, but we observe a more balanced workload across nurses. We, however, also see that this inevitably increases the waiting times of the patients: the expected total waiting time increases by around 6%, demonstrating the trade-off between the overtime and waiting time related criteria.

5.3 Improvement over the Baseline Schedule

In the previous section, we discussed how an OCU manager can use SMIP-1 variants to obtain schedules that reflect the priorities of the OCU. In this section, we compare the schedules obtained by mathematical models (SMIP-1 and SMIP-6) with the baseline schedule that is currently used in practice. Recall that in the OCU we consider, the head nurse allocates patients to four main appointment slots: two in the morning (08:00 and 10:30) and two in the afternoon (13:00 and 15:30). Patients with longer expected treatment durations are assigned to the first slot of each shift to minimize overtime, while those with shorter treatments are placed in the second slot.

We consider an instance with 8 patients, 4 chairs and 2 nurses, whose infusion time data is provided in Table 5.5. Based on their expected infusion durations, Patients 1, 3, 5, and 7 are allocated to the 8:00 am slot, while the remaining are allocated to the 10:30 am slot of the half-day schedule.

Table 5.5 Infusion durations in scenarios (minutes)

	Scenarios				
Patients	1	2	3	4	5
1	105	118	123	117	118
2	21	27	127	24	22
3	40	153	128	55	111
4	22	114	98	32	117
5	96	118	90	120	139
6	150	20	38	129	24
7	130	42	120	124	51
8	64	29	139	143	23

Table 5.6 Comparison of SMIP solutions with the baseline schedule used by the OCC. All times are reported in minutes (*WT* Waiting time, *OT* Overtime)

	SMIP-1										Baseline									
Scenario	WT								OT		WT								OT	
	1	2	3	4	5	6	7	8	1	2	1	2	3	4	5	6	7	8	1	2
1	0	0	0	0	0	0	0	0	6	0	15	15	0	0	0	0	15	15	0	75
2	0	0	0	0	0	0	0	0	0	37	15	18	0	0	0	0	15	15	39	0
3	9	0	0	2	0	0	0	7	0	34	15	30	0	0	0	0	15	15	82	0
4	13	0	0	2	0	0	0	0	31	0	15	15	0	0	0	0	15	15	0	83
5	0	0	0	0	0	0	0	0	40	0	15	15	0	0	0	0	15	15	0	42
	SMIP-6 (G=0)										SMIP-1 (L=35)									
Scenario	WT								OT		WT								OT	
	1	2	3	4	5	6	7	8	1	2	1	2	3	4	5	6	7	8	1	2
1	0	0	0	0	0	0	0	0	6	0	2	0	6	2	0	0	0	0	0	10
2	0	0	0	0	0	0	0	0	19	0	0	0	0	0	0	0	0	0	0	33
3	0	0	0	0	0	0	0	0	0	67	7	0	0	14	0	0	0	17	0	33
4	0	0	0	0	0	0	0	0	62	0	11	0	30	16	0	0	0	3	31	0
5	0	0	0	0	0	0	0	0	19	0	0	0	0	0	0	0	0	1	35	0

We obtain schedules by solving variants of SMIP-1 under a time limit of 200 seconds. Table 5.6 presents the resulting waiting times and overtimes. The first schedule is generated by solving SMIP-1 with the weight parameter λ set to 0.3, a very high maximum allowable overtime per nurse in any scenario (90 minutes), and no constraints on the inequality of waiting time allocations. For comparison, we also include the performance metrics of two schedules generated under stricter fairness and overtime constraints: SMIP-6 with a Gini threshold of zero for waiting time allocations and SMIP-1 with a maximum overtime limit of 35 minutes per nurse, respectively.

Since the baseline schedule lacks information on the realized assignment decisions, we approximate them by assuming optimal patient–nurse and patient–chair assignments given

Table 5.7 Percentage improvements of model solutions over the baseline schedule

	Expected total waiting time	Expected total overtime
SMIP-1	89.62	53.89
SMIP-6 (G=0)	100	46.11
SMIP-1 (L=35)	65.72	55.76

the appointment times. To estimate this, we fix the appointment times in SMIP-1 and solve for the best possible assignment, using a one-hour time limit.

Note that the SMIP-1 and SMIP-6 solutions are not the optimal ones; but those obtained with a 200 seconds of time limit. Hence their performances constitute lower bounds for the performances of the corresponding optimal schedules. Yet, even these schedules outperform the baseline schedule with respect to both waiting times of patients and overtimes of nurses. Table 5.7 summarizes the percentage improvements gained by mathematical model solutions over the baseline schedule.

We observe an almost 90% reduction in total expected waiting time and around 54% improvement in total expected overtime in the SMIP-1 solution, compared to the baseline schedule. This notable improvement mainly comes from the flexibility in appointment time assignments brought by the model, as opposed to the relatively rigid half-day arrangements of the baseline schedule. Ensuring equality in waiting times, SMIP-6 solution results in an approximately 17% increase in the expected overtime compared to the variant with no fairness restrictions (SMIP-1), but it still brings a 46% improvement over the baseline schedule.

Lastly, controlling the upper bound on overtimes (L) brings a reduction in the maximum overtime faced by a nurse in any scenario, which also improves the total expected overtime. When compared to the SMIP-1 solution with L=90, SMIP-1 (L=35) has 4% less total expected overtime. Yet, this leads to a 230% increase (from 6.6 to 21.8 minutes) in expected waiting time. Still, this solution improves the baseline schedule by approximately 66% and 56% in terms of expected total waiting time and total overtime, respectively.

References

1. Çelik, B., Gul, S., & Karsu, Ö. (2025). Maintaining fairness in stochastic chemotherapy scheduling. *Omega, 137*, 103338.
2. Demir, N. B., Gul, S., & Çelik, M. (2021). A stochastic programming approach for chemotherapy appointment scheduling. *Naval Research Logistics, 68*(1), 112–133.
3. Gul, S. (2024). Nursing care flexibility in chemotherapy appointment scheduling. *Flexible Services and Manufacturing Journal, 36*, 918–945.
4. Karakaya, S., Gul, S., & Çelik, M. (2023). Stochastic scheduling of chemotherapy appointments considering patient acuity levels. *European Journal of Operational Research, 305*(2), 902–916.
5. Ozyuksel, E. D., et al. (2025). Coordinating oncologist appointments with chemotherapy treatments under uncertainty. *Computers & Industrial Engineering, 204*, 111123.

Conclusion and Future Directions 6

6.1 Conclusion

As cancer incidence rate continues to rise worldwide and treatment success improves, the demand for oncology services is accelerating. This growing demand, which already exceeds existing service capacity, underscores the need for more effective resource utilization strategies. Operations Research (OR) approaches can provide valuable support in this regard, particularly in chemotherapy services, which remain a cornerstone of cancer care across all disease stages. Given the strong shift toward outpatient delivery, optimizing patient flow in outpatient chemotherapy units (OCUs) is especially critical. Improved scheduling of OCU operations can play a decisive role in increasing utilization of OCU resources and enhancing patient satisfaction.

In a typical OCU, patient flow spans several steps and resources before discharge. After registration, patients undergo lab tests by phlebotomists and meet oncologists for consultation. Once treatment is approved, pharmacists prepare the chemotherapy drugs. Patients are then seated for chemotherapy, which begins with premedication requiring full nurse involvement and continues with infusion, where the nurse's role is primarily monitoring.

Patients visit OCUs multiple times during their therapy, as chemotherapy treatment typically follows a cyclical structure in which drug administration days alternate with recovery periods across several weeks. Each patient is given a chemotherapy regimen that clearly defines the drugs, their timing, and dosage levels at the beginning of their therapy. Maintaining this schedule is crucial, as early treatment raises toxicity risks while delays reduce dose intensity and effectiveness.

In the first phase of chemotherapy scheduling (i.e., chemotherapy treatment planning), patients are assigned treatment days based on the constraints of their prescribed regimen. In the second phase (i.e., chemotherapy appointment scheduling), appointment times are

S. Gul, Ö. Karsu, *Chemotherapy Appointment Scheduling*, Synthesis Lectures on Operations Research and Applications, https://doi.org/10.1007/978-3-032-11552-2_6

set for each daily patient list. When generating a complete schedule, multiple factors must be considered, with three requiring particular attention: uncertainty, fairness, and care coordination.

In the chemotherapy treatment planning phase, uncertainty in patient arrivals and treatment durations is an important factor to consider. Treatment days for each patient are determined in accordance with the rest periods specified in their regimen. Time windows are typically pre-defined for each treatment before assigning patients to days. Given the long horizons of treatment cycles and the dynamic arrival of requests, rolling horizon approaches are often used to obtain solutions. Key performance measures include penalties for overtime, idle time, and deviations from time windows.

In the chemotherapy appointment scheduling (CAS) phase, three key decisions must be made: setting patient appointment times, assigning nurses, and assigning chairs. Although the use of fixed-time slots is common both in practice and in the literature, employing a decision support tool makes it possible to schedule appointments at any integer time. This flexibility can help reduce unnecessary idle time in the OCU and minimize patient waiting, which may otherwise be worsened by rigid slot-based scheduling.

When assigning patients to nurses, the most realistic approach is to account for differences in nurse skill levels and to define an acuity level for each patient. Patients are then assigned only to eligible nurses, while ensuring that each nurse's capacity in terms of total acuity is respected throughout the treatment day. Although both practice and the literature commonly assume that a nurse can treat up to four patients simultaneously during infusion, incorporating patient acuity leads to more balanced nurse–patient assignments and, consequently, improved schedule performance. In addition, assignments should also reflect the differing levels of nursing care required during premedication compared with infusion. Finally, total workload should be balanced across nurses to promote both fairness and efficiency.

The degree of flexibility in the nursing care delivery system is also an important consideration in nurse assignment. In a fully flexible system (i.e., functional care delivery), patients can be assigned to any eligible nurse at a given treatment visit, which means their nurse may change from one visit to another. In an inflexible system (i.e., primary care delivery), each patient is consistently assigned to the same nurse across all visits. A partially flexible system lies between these two extremes: patients are preferably assigned to their primary nurse, but reassignment to other nurses remains possible when needed. Fully flexible systems promote efficiency, whereas inflexible systems prioritize continuity of care and, consequently, treatment quality. A partially flexible system seeks to balance the trade-off between these two objectives.

Since chairs are identical, assigning them upon patient arrival at the OCU generally results in more efficient schedules than assigning them in advance at the time of appointment setting. Similarly, if nurses are assumed to be identical, their assignments can also be deferred until patient arrival.

In CAS models, infusion duration is the most critical random parameter, whereas premedication duration is often treated as deterministic. Common sources of deviation from estimated infusion durations include early termination of infusion, adverse drug reactions or complications, last-minute drug changes due to revised clinical assessments, and issues related to drug availability.

When care coordination between oncologist consultations and chemotherapy appointments is considered, treatment approval status following the consultation becomes another important source of uncertainty. Although not commonly investigated in CAS models, patient unpunctuality also deserves to be modeled as a stochastic factor.

Patient waiting time and overtime are the most relevant performance measures in CAS models, as they reflect both patient and provider satisfaction. When integrated scheduling of oncologist consultations and chemotherapy appointments is considered, makespan may serve as an alternative to overtime. Additional important measures include balance in the instantaneous nurse workload in terms of patient acuity levels, as well as balance in the overall daily nurse workload, particularly when treatment quality and fairness are prioritized. Finally, the number of handovers between nurses during chemotherapy is another meaningful performance measure in CAS models.

Two-stage stochastic mixed-integer programming (SMIP) is the most commonly used modeling framework for representing the CAS problem under uncertainty. These models are typically solved using decomposition methods. Alternatively, scenario reduction techniques can be applied, allowing the models to be solved directly without the need for decomposition.

As examples of SMIP formulations for the CAS problem, we present several models adapted from the literature, including those by Demir et al., Gul, Karakaya et al., Ozyuksel et al., and Celik et al. [2, 4, 6, 7, 9, 11]. We begin with a base model, which represents the first developed approach for generating a complete daily schedule for an OCU under uncertainty in treatment durations. Since this model does not explicitly account for balancing nurses' total daily workloads, managing their instantaneous workload, incorporating different forms of nursing care flexibility, coordinating oncologist appointments with chemotherapy treatments, or integrating fairness measures, we subsequently present extensions of this model that address each of these aspects.

As in most problems arising in healthcare delivery, fairness is a key criterion in the CAS problem. The notion of fairness, however, is inherently context-dependent, and there exists no universally accepted definition of what constitutes a *perfectly fair* allocation. Nevertheless, the literature offers effective methodological frameworks for quantifying and incorporating fairness into decision-making models.

A structured approach to conceptualizing fairness involves addressing three key dimensions: (1) what is being allocated, (2) to whom, and (3) how fairness is operationalized. The first dimension pertains to the benefit or burden under consideration. In the context of chemotherapy scheduling, common burdens include patient waiting times and nurse workloads. It is important to note that these quantities are not directly allocated in a deterministic manner, as would be the case, for example, with monetary resources. Rather, scheduling and assignment decisions are made that indirectly result in these outcomes.

Accordingly, fairness is sought with respect to the resulting outcomes, rather than the input decisions themselves. This further justifies the use of optimization tools in CAS settings.

The second dimension concerns the recipients of the allocation. Fairness concerns over waiting times is related to patients, who are the primary beneficiaries of care, whereas workload fairness pertains to nurses, as service providers. In many models, the entities for whom fairness is sought are treated to be indistinguishable, in line with the anonymity axiom from the inequality measurement literature. This axiom stipulates that fairness evaluations should be invariant to the identities of the individuals involved.

The third dimension involves the operationalization of fairness within an optimization framework. This requires a quantitative assessment of fairness across possible allocation vectors, typically through the use of fairness-related objective or constraint functions. These functions can be broadly categorized into two classes. The first includes spread-based functions, which evaluate the dispersion in allocations and are generally invariant to efficiency, i.e., the total amount of the resource or burden allocated. The second class includes social welfare functions or equitable aggregation functions, which jointly consider efficiency and equity, enabling an aggregated evaluation. Incorporating such functions into mathematical models enables the decision-maker to balance competing objectives, such as minimizing waiting times or overtimes while ensuring equitable treatment of all patients or staff.

One key challenge that arises when ensuring fairness in CAS is the stochastic nature of treatment durations, particularly with regard to infusion times, which introduces significant uncertainty in outcomes. This uncertainty complicates the process, as the actual outcomes may deviate considerably from their expected values. Optimizing for fairness in expectation alone may result in undesirable or inequitable realizations under specific scenarios. Scheduling solutions must therefore account not just for average fairness, but also for robustness across a range of possible realizations. We illustrate the use of example fairness functions in SMIP models, that would ensure a desired degree of fairness in all resulting waiting time allocations.

Finally, we illustrate the dynamics of the CAS problem through a case study based on real-world data. The case study is developed using operational data and scheduling practices from the OCU of Hacettepe University Oncology Hospital in Ankara, Turkey. By analyzing infusion duration data, we are able to generate realistic scenario sets for subsequent experimental evaluations. We then assess the performance gains achievable through a stochastic optimization approach, comparing it against the current scheduling method employed in practice. The results clearly highlight the advantages of incorporating optimization techniques into this inherently complex problem. By calibrating model parameters to reflect institutional priorities and stakeholder preferences, the proposed approach yields schedules that significantly outperform the baseline across all key performance indicators—namely, total patient waiting time, total overtime, and equity considerations for both patients and nurses.

6.2 Directions for Future Work

Although several aspects of chemotherapy scheduling have been studied in recent years, numerous open problems remain to be explored. In this section, we first outline possible future research directions, and then discuss practical steps that could enhance the prevalence and impact of OR techniques and the findings of OR-based studies in real-world applications. Before presenting future research directions, we emphasize that future studies must explicitly account for uncertainty in infusion durations. Therefore, in all of the open directions we propose, stochastic infusion durations are assumed.

While this book has primarily focused on the CAS phase, the chemotherapy treatment planning phase also poses important challenges for future research. For instance, stochastic dynamic programming (SDP) formulations that jointly capture uncertainty in both appointment request arrivals and infusion durations are needed. In addition, this phase should also account for the coordination of oncologist consultations with chemotherapy appointments.

In the subsequent phase of chemotherapy scheduling (i.e., CAS), recent studies have examined the coordinated scheduling of oncologist consultations and chemotherapy treatments under uncertainty [5, 8, 11]. To realistically represent this integrated setting, a CAS model should capture: (i) three patient flow types—patients requiring both consultation and chemotherapy, consultation-only, and chemotherapy-only; (ii) appointment-time decisions for both stages; and (iii) day-of nurse and chair assignments that are made after patients arrive.

The framework can be extended to incorporate pre-chemotherapy blood testing, with two clinically relevant variants: (1) laboratory tests completed on the day before chemotherapy and (2) tests performed on the same day. Even though these pathways have been examined in empirical studies based on manually created schedules, their relative merits should also be assessed using the performance of optimal schedules.

Uncertainty due to patient unpunctuality remains under-modeled. To our knowledge, there is no stochastic programming (SP) or SDP formulation for CAS that explicitly treats unpunctuality, despite its clear impact on the utilization of key resources and waiting time/overtime values.

Ensuring fairness in highly stochastic problems remains significantly underexplored. The way fairness is quantified can greatly shape decision-making, with major implications for balancing workloads and achieving equality in outcomes such as waiting times. Exploring how different fairness modeling frameworks impact these outcomes—and analyzing how various fairness metrics influence scheduling and assignment policies—is a valuable direction for further research. Multi-objective programming approaches that incorporate multiple fairness and/or efficiency metrics offer promising tools in this context. However, ensuring fairness in stochastic environments is particularly challenging, as it is closely tied to the risk preferences of decision-makers. Assuming risk neutrality and focusing solely on expected outcomes can lead to highly undesirable—and potentially life-threatening—allocations, especially in critical domains like healthcare. To address this, stochastic and robust optimization techniques may offer more equitable and reliable solutions, enabling efficiency and fairness to be maintained even under uncertainty.

While entities are often assumed to be indistinguishable in many fairness-oriented models, there are important contexts in healthcare, where individuals differ across key dimensions. Patients, for instance, may vary in terms of clinical urgency or overall health status, which in turn influences their tolerance to delays or waiting times. In such settings, achieving fairness may require the *unequal treatment of unequals*, deeming conventional fairness formulations based on symmetry or anonymity inadequate. How fairness should be modeled in the presence of such heterogeneity remains an open question within the CAS domain. This underscores the need for modeling frameworks that offer flexibility in accommodating heterogeneous populations, and that can operationalize fairness in ways that are sensitive to contextual differences across individuals or groups.

Finally, most SP-based CAS studies solve instances of roughly 8–9 patients because of computational complexity. Such models are well suited to small "pod" configurations (e.g., 2–3 nurses serving 3–5 chairs) where rooms can be scheduled independently. For larger, open-plan OCUs where many patients are treated in a common area, more scalable approaches are needed. One promising direction is the use of scenario reduction methods, since the complexity of CAS models is highly dependent on the number of scenarios considered. By replacing the original scenario set with a smaller but representative subset, much larger problem instances—involving more patients, chairs, and nurses—can potentially be solved.

Scenario reduction methods are broadly classified into two categories: (1) distribution-based methods and (2) problem-based methods. Distribution-based methods assess the similarity or distance between scenarios based solely on input parameter values, and then select a representative subset of scenarios according to these measures. In contrast, problem-based methods evaluate the similarity of scenarios with respect to their associated objective values. To obtain these objective values, a set of feasible solutions must first be generated and then assessed under each scenario. Although this approach is more computationally demanding than distribution-based methods, it typically yields scenario subsets that more accurately represent the original set, since it leverages problem-specific information. Consequently, the latter has received increasing attention in recent SP studies and offers a particularly promising avenue for the development of new problem-based techniques [1, 3, 10, 12].

Since chemotherapy scheduling problems are highly stochastic, the development of fast and effective computational tools that can be used in practice is essential. Equally important is the design of user-friendly software and interface systems that make such tools accessible to practitioners, reducing the gap between complex optimization models and everyday clinical decision making. Another important direction is the creation of frameworks that simplify sensitivity and trade-off analyses, enabling practitioners to better understand how different modeling choices impact patient- and provider-related measures. Advances in forecasting and learning systems also hold promise, particularly for improving the prediction of infusion durations. More accurate forecasts would allow for more refined scenario sets, thereby improving the overall performance of stochastic models in practice.

References

1. Bertsimas, D., & Mundru, N. (2023). Optimization-based scenario reduction for data-driven two-stage stochastic optimization. *Operations Research, 71*(4), 1343–1361.
2. Çelik, B., Gul, S.,, & Karsu, Ö. (2025). Maintaining fairness in stochastic chemotherapy scheduling. *Omega, 137*, 103338.
3. Dağıstanlı, G. (2025). *Planning and scheduling of chemotherapy operations*. Ph.D. Thesis. Ankara, Türkiye: Middle East Technical University.
4. Demir, N. B., Gul, S., & Çelik, M. (2021). A stochastic programming approach for chemotherapy appointment scheduling. *Naval Research Logistics, 68*(1), 112–133.
5. Garaix, T., Rostami, S., & Xie, X. (2020). Daily outpatient chemotherapy appointment scheduling with random deferrals. *Flexible Services and Manufacturing Journal, 32*, 129–153.
6. Gul, S. (2021). Chemotherapy appointment scheduling under uncertainty by considering workload balance among nurses. *Pamukkale Üniversitesi Mühendislik Bilimleri Dergisi, 27*(4), 570–578. ISSN: 1300-7009.
7. Gul, S. (2024). Nursing care flexibility in chemotherapy appointment scheduling. *Flexible Services and Manufacturing Journal, 36*, 918–945.
8. Haghi, M., et al. (2023). Integrated consultation and chemotherapy scheduling with stochastic treatment times. *Journal of the Operational Research Society, 74*(9), 2012–2027.
9. Karakaya, S., Gul, S., & Çelik, M. (2023). Stochastic scheduling of chemotherapy appointments considering patient acuity levels. *European Journal of Operational Research, 305*(2), 902–916.
10. Keutchayan, J., Ortmann, J., & Rei, W. (2023). Problem-driven scenario clustering in stochastic optimization. *Computational Management Science, 20*, 13.
11. Ozyuksel, E. D., et al. (2025). Coordinating oncologist appointments with chemotherapy treatments under uncertainty. *Computers & Industrial Engineering, 204*, 111123.
12. Prochazka, V., & Wallace, S. W. (2020). Scenario tree construction driven by heuristic solutions of the optimization problem. *Computational Management Science, 17*(2), 277–307.

MIX
Papier aus verantwortungsvollen Quellen
Paper from responsible sources
FSC® C105338

If you have any concerns about our products,
you can contact us on
ProductSafety@springernature.com

In case Publisher is established outside the EU,
the EU authorized representative is:
Springer Nature Customer Service Center GmbH
Europaplatz 3, 69115 Heidelberg, Germany

Printed by Libri Plureos GmbH
in Hamburg, Germany